8 (Really Creative) Ways to Save!

Kristin King

8 (Really Creative) Ways to Save!

Kristin King

Copyright © 2015 by Kristin King

K L J Creative, LLC

Dedication

To all the timid savers out there who are ready to fund the life of your dreams:

I hope this book gives you encouragement for the journey and enough fresh ideas to help you save more than ever before!

Contents

Foreword: Embarking on This Journey

Let me just get this confession out of the way first. I am writing this book for me. I am writing this book because I need it. I am only hopeful that in the end, my journey will be helpful to someone else. Maybe my mistakes and successes at saving money will encourage others to realize that they too can fund and live the life they've always dreamed about.

It's time. I sit here on my couch at the beginning of a new year and I know that I've got to get intense about saving money. Not just because I would like to retire wealthy someday (which I would, no shame!), but more important, because I have many dreams to live. All of those dreams require little green rectangles that come in quantities of 1's, 2's, 5's, 10's, 20's, 50's, and 100's.

You might wonder who am I to be writing a book on savings. I'm no money expert, that's for sure. There are times in my life when I am able to save money with the best of them. And then there are other times when I look at my monthly budget and wring my hands, wondering where in the world our income went to so quickly. My family is not out of debt. As of this writing, I have a small portion of a student loan left, as well as a car payment each month. But I want to be debt-free.

I've seen the rewards that come to those who work hard and save hard. Take the example of my parents, who made their money stretch on my dad's income alone so my mom could stay at home with my sister and me. That sacrifice required them to save and scrimp when others were spending, but it netted an incalculable reward of having a mom who came to every school function and was always there to take us to and pick us up from school.

I've also seen examples of families and couples who didn't put forth any effort to save. They spent all they had and more, going into debt when they didn't have the cash. I've watched their possessions be sold and their homes put up for foreclosure. I've seen children so grateful for a simple home-cooked meal because their parents had no money set aside for groceries. I've seen the devastation that comes when people don't take time or expend any effort to put away money for the future. Because the future always comes, whether or not we are ready for it.

The biggest lesson I am learning about saving is that it might be painful at the moment to "go without," but in the end, it yields freedom. Freedom to live without the bondage of debt. Freedom to try new things. Freedom to raise up the next generation and mold our children into responsible money managers. Ask any prisoner: Once you get a taste of freedom, it's harder going back to the chains.

And so I am embarking on this journey to save. It's the beginning of the year and I would like to challenge myself to save more than I ever have before by the time I mark off December 31 on the calendar. I would like to recognize some of my dreams this year like finally, *finally* kicking my student loan of nine years to the curb. I would like to go on a special birthday trip with my husband and family to New York City. And both of those dreams can be realized through smart and methodical saving techniques.

But, not just any saving will do. I'm not going to start throwing dollars into a cookie jar for a rainy day. (Besides, where would the cookies go?) I'm going to try some creative ways to save and see which methods work best for me. After all, what do I have to lose? I'm sure some will work better than others and some won't fit my lifestyle. But I'm fairly certain they will all help me save more than ever before.

Won't you join me on this journey to saving the creative way in order to fund your dreams? Let's get started.

Kristin King
January 18, 2015

Chapter 1: Funding Your Dreams and Finding Your Why

Have you taken the time to dream lately? I mean, really sit down and think about your ideal life.

What does it look like?

Where do you live?

What do you do for a living?

Who is there with you?

How is your dream life different from the reality you find yourself living now?

Chances are, your reality and your dream life don't exactly match up. There are probably some things you could see yourself doing, if you only had the money. This book is all about "finding" the money you need to fund your dreams. It's not about getting a job or boosting your income, although both of those things will inevitably help you save more.

It's about harnessing what you do make, paying yourself first, and using some creative and downright sneaky savings techniques to help you retain more of your take-home pay. Sounds nice, right? I promise, it isn't some pipe dream. All it takes is a little creativity, a willingness to delay instant gratification for future rewards, and a vision of your dreams coming to pass. Let's start with the big "W," your why.

Finding the Why

It was one of the most thought-provoking professional development seminars I had ever been required to sit through. As a high school chorus teacher, I could think of a thousand other things I needed to be working on during preplanning week, and yet I was sitting at a required training for all teachers. But instead of having to listen to another lecture on testing or the state of our education system, the principal played a video clip of Simon Sinek talking about finding the "why."

Sinek's premise is simple, yet powerful: you won't find true motivation to do anything and complete it unless you understand why you are doing it. He says to "start with why" (Simon Sinek, "Start With Why," YouTube), and that will get you going to answer all the other "whats, whens, and hows."

As I listened to the message, I thought about my own why for working with those high school students. I love music and wanted to pass along my delight and passion for singing to them. It seemed I wasn't the only teacher who discovered the importance of finding her why that day. Our school was struggling and had been for the past four years. With a diverse mix of cultures, mostly socioeconomically disadvantaged kids coming to our school, our standardized test grades continued to be dismal. So many students just didn't care about school, and their parents at home didn't seem to care if they finished or not.

The teachers and administration were fighting a tidal wave of apathetic mindset. But that day of preplanning, we were given a boost to remember "why" we were there in the first place, and to hold that "why" in our heads as the school year progressed. It didn't make the year any easier. In fact, we were in so much trouble that the heads of the district took up camp in our school, basically leaving an unsettling feeling on campus. It started to feel a little like *Hunger Games* there.

But, by the end of the year, the school made an incredible, unprecedented turnaround. We had, as a team, banded together and pulled the school grade up into the better-than-average range! Was it a miracle? Someone looking in from the outside might say yes, but I would counter and say it was a lot of hard work and knowing why we were teaching those kids, day in and day out.

Finding your why is critical to get you started on any goal, big or small. If you say you want to lose twenty pounds and then set out to do it, the first time an obstacle in the form of a hot, glazed donut presents itself, you're going to fail if you don't know why you're trying to lose weight. It's the same concept with your money. If you're not accustomed to saving regularly, you might start out strong, but without a clear reason why you're saving, it will be too easy to quit the first time you're tempted to blow your savings.

So, the beginning of this book is going to start out fun! In fact, this might be the most fun you have, at least while we go through the process of actually putting money aside for savings (don't say I didn't warn you). Below is a summary of the three-step process this book will guide you through:

Step 1: Describe Your Dream Life	
Goal #1 to save for	Goal #2 to save for

Step 2: Save using 8 Creative Ways	
Tedious, sometimes boring, hard work	More hard work, but making progress!

Step 3: Fund Your Dream Life!	
Pay cash for Goal #1!	Pay cash for Goal #2!

To begin the process, we will start out by making a dream list, or, in other words, defining our "why." **Please do not skip this step!** It is your key to staying motivated when we get into step #2, the nitty-gritty of saving. This is where we employ the eight creative ways of saving that are detailed in this book.

You might consider testing each of them and then choosing the ones that worked best for you or create your own variations. After some time and some sweat and the savings you've accumulated, you get to go back to the fun part again, only this part is going to be seeing the realization of step #1. Step #3 is getting to live the two dreams you defined in step #1 by paying for your goals!

Any time you feel like it's too hard to save money, or you'd rather have a designer coffee drink instead of putting aside that five dollar bill, return to your goal list and think how good it will feel to finally drive that paid-for car or go on that exotic vacation you've been collecting brochures for.

It's time to channel your inner artist. Don't worry if you can't really draw. Me either! Let's just pretend we're back in elementary school art class for a moment and everyone's work is good (even the picture that is indecipherable).

Defining Your Goals

Think for a moment about two goals you would love to accomplish tomorrow *if money was no concern*. You might wonder why I only say two goals, but we're just getting started. I'm sure I could come up with a whole list of things I'd like to save for, but more than likely, I would take one look at that list, get overwhelmed, and tuck it away somewhere safe for another day. So, I'll start with two goals, because once I have some traction and those two goals are realized, I can work toward saving for the next two goals, and so on. Baby steps here, people!

On a blank sheet of paper, jot down those two goals however you'd like. You can use fancy script or make each letter a different color or make fun cartoon letters. It doesn't matter. If you're brave enough, doodle a picture of each goal being realized. No one has to see this picture but you! The main idea is getting your two "whys" down on paper and out of your head. When you're in the midst of saving, you can pull this paper out from wherever you're hiding it (so the rest of the household doesn't find it and commit you), and remind yourself that you have goals! And you're not going to stop saving until you reach them.

My two starting goals for this project are funding my New York City birthday trip and paying off my car. So naturally, my doodle paper is going to have a drawing of the Statue of Liberty and a drawing of my Ford Fusion car that I drive. I also have some pretty fancy Sharpie markers in a wide variety of colors, so I'll use those to embellish my goal sheet. You might use stickers, magazine cutouts, inspirational quotes, or glitter. It doesn't really matter as long as you make it your own and you get inspired every time you look at it. And remember, no one else needs to see it, unless you want him or her to.

Once your goal sheet is complete, there is one more thing to do before you jump into saving. Clear out five minutes of your day and visualize yourself having saved up and paying for those goals. For my New York trip goal, I picture myself stepping off a plane in New York City with a purse full of spending money and a big grin on my face. I picture walking around with my family in Central Park on a hot summer day, sipping an iced coffee. For my car goal, I picture writing the check for my last car payment, years before I would have actually paid it off if I had just made the minimum payment each month. I try to imagine what it would feel like driving my toddler son around in a paid-for car. I see in my mind's eye the deed to my car, arriving in the mailbox.

When I think about my savings goals in this way, it makes them almost tangible to me. I am so motivated, I can hardly wait to get started. And I know that if I work hard enough and pile away enough cash, I will one day be *living* those scenarios I just played out in my head. It's possible for me and it's possible for you.

Funding a New Bank

If you're going to start saving money, you're going to need a place to store your newfound cash. In my opinion, there are two good options for this: one is a savings account at whatever bank you use and the other is your own personal "bank" in the privacy of your home. Depending on how well you can handle money being around you (actual paperbacks, that is) and not be tempted to dip into it every time your friends want to go to dinner, one option will probably appeal to you over the other.

If you can't see a dollar bill without spending it, it's probably best to open a traditional savings account at your local bank. If you already have a savings account, see if you can link it to your checking account. That way, you can transfer money effortlessly at the touch of a few keystrokes. Some banks will let you name your savings account. I recommend coming up with a creative name that motivates you when you see it. It could be "The Dream-n-Save Account" or "Life Goal Savings" or anything else you want to call it.

Once you have a savings account set up and ready to use, make a promise to yourself that you will not dip into it **unless** you have a true emergency and you can't pay cash for it any other way, or you have enough saved up to fund one of your current dream goals. Don't worry about finding the best interest rate for your savings account because to be honest, savings accounts are not about earning you interest. That's what your investments are for. Your savings account will require YOU to do the work by putting money in; the bank's only job is to store it for you and keep you from getting to it easily. However, do look for a bank that doesn't charge you a monthly fee to store your money. That seems ridiculous to me that I would give someone my business and my money for safekeeping and in return I have to pay a fee. No, thanks.

There is another option if you can't or don't want to use a traditional savings account through a bank. You can save and fund your own bank, right in your home. Several years ago, I picked up a cute little moneybox at Target in the dollar section. I decided to use it to store all my earnings from summer piano lessons. Fast-forward nine months and my husband and I were getting ready to go on a trip to Washington, DC. Instead of making a trip to the ATM, I surprised my husband with spending cash straight out of my moneybox. I hadn't told him I was saving my lesson funds, and he was more than pleased with the $500 in cash I presented to him.

I affectionately named that box the "Bank of Kristin," and I still use it to put away cash. I do dip into it from time to time, but it has worked out great for us during the past few years. I also have a peace of mind that in case of an apocalyptic disaster (my husband believes it will be a zombie apocalypse), I don't have to worry about getting to an ATM. I can just grab some cash and go.

If the idea of having your own liquid savings account appeals to you, all you need to do is designate a box or envelope and start loading it with cash, using the ideas in the next section. You will be surprised how quickly the cash will start adding up as you make an effort to save for your goals. It's also fun to pull out the money and count it once in a while!

If you fear you'll have issues keeping cash on-hand without spending it, can you trust your spouse or partner to keep it for you? If neither of you can keep cash around, it's probably a good idea to use the first option and open a traditional savings account. Either way will work with the eight ways to save. One will require you to drive to the bank every so often (which you probably already do anyway) or access your account electronically.

Making Savings Fun

Sometimes when you're in the middle of a savings plan, it's just not fun. You don't know if you can stand one more microwave meal in lieu of eating out at the newest

21

posh restaurant with your friends. When the going gets tough, you need to surround yourself with fun visual cues that motivate you and get you through.

Any time I'm trying to drop a couple of pounds, I've found it's particularly motivating to me to see my progress on paper with one of those thermometer goal charts. You know, the one where you color in starting at the bottom until you have filled it all the way up to the top. That kind of visual cue can also easily be adapted for savings goals. If the chart has increments in ten and you are trying to save $2,000, you can write benchmarks for every $200 you save. You can easily find a blank thermometer goal form by searching for it online. Save a copy to your computer and then you can access it each time you start a new savings goal.

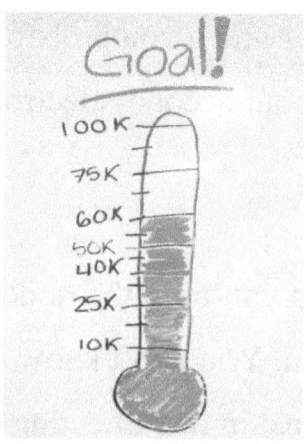

Another idea is creating a vision board. This is where you place pictures, inspiring quotes, or even drawings of your life, as you want it to be. Maybe you already have a vision board for other areas of your life. Could you add a picture or quote that represents your current savings goals? Vision boards are most inspiring when they're placed somewhere you will see them daily. If you have kids, get them involved in helping you create a vision board for your savings goals. It will be both motivating and a fun art project for the family.

I have always loved paper, since I was a little kid. Growing up, I had a giant box divided into four segments, holding every shape, size, and color of paper. Naturally as an adult, I use Post-It notes every day. One of the ways I can keep myself motivated during my savings journey is to write and post encouraging quotes and sayings around my house, on my desk at work, and in my car. If sticky notes aren't your thing, maybe there is something else that visually motivates you.

Another idea is to decorate the box or envelope that holds your savings. You can be as creative as you'd like. Maybe you want to bedazzle your moneybox. Grab a hot glue gun and get to work. You could turn it into an item you're saving toward, such as a small replica of the car you want to buy. You can use bright markers to outline your savings goal right on the envelope. The idea is to make the box or envelope an inviting temporary "storage unit" for your cash that you feel compelled to fill up often.

By the end of this chapter, you should have completed the first step of this process, which is defining your "why" or naming the first two goals you'd like to save for. Now that we've firmly established our dreams and had a little fun in the process, there's nothing left to do but to dive into saving money, using an arsenal of creative ideas.

Chapter 2: Surefire Savings!

Disclaimer: I know I promised you eight really creative ways to save, and what you are about to read is not creative at all. Stick with me; there's a method to my madness. I couldn't write a book about saving money and not include one absolute surefire way to save more money than you have in the past. I'm not going to lie: this method is boring, but if you don't try any of the other tips in this book and only use this one, you will grow your savings account. I promise we'll get to the unique savings tips in the next chapter.

Automation, Baby!

It was the summer of 2011, and after three long, tedious years of trying to be hired as a music teacher in my county, I finally got my break. I interviewed at two different schools in one day: a middle school and a high school. As it turned out, both schools offered me a position. I had gone from looking for whatever I could find to having the power to decide which job I wanted more. I chose to take the high school chorus teacher position and practically floated through the new teacher training.

At long last, my hustle and hard work had paid off! The last day of training, I sat through the financial workshop, which included setting up my paycheck with direct deposit. On impulse, I decided to designate $50 from each paycheck to go to my personal savings account and the rest to go into my joint checking account with my husband.

That was four years ago. Even though I now only teach part-time, I still have $50 automatically deposited into that same savings account every pay period. I get paid twice a month. I went from having $700 in the savings account when I started teaching to more than $4,000 last year. Then in November, I decided I wanted to make a huge dent in the student loan still hanging over my head, so I withdrew $3,000 to pay the loan, leaving $1,000 for my starter emergency fund (courtesy of Dave Ramsey's awesome Financial Peace University program).

Even though my savings dwindled, so did the debt. As a result of that move, I now have two more payments on my loan as I write this chapter, and then I am done with student loans forever! I can't tell you how amazing that feels! If I hadn't impulsively decided to automate my savings when I got hired as a teacher four years ago, I wouldn't have been able to throw down a huge chunk of money on my loan. Sure, I would have had an extra $50 every pay period, but what would I have to show for it? Probably not much. For me, $50 is just enough that it helps me feel that I'm moving forward with my savings goals a little each year, but it's not big enough to cause a significant loss in my take-home pay.

The title of this chapter is "Surefire Savings." That is what you'll get if you automate a portion of your income to go directly to your savings account every time you get a paycheck. In the last chapter, I recommended using a traditional savings account at your bank or keeping cash on hand in your home. What I didn't tell you is that I do both.

For my surefire savings plan, I'm already using direct deposit to the bank, so there is no reason to make extra work for myself by withdrawing the cash. Besides, if I brought $50 cash home with me every other week, I don't know that I could keep from dipping into it for a little purchase now and then. Having the money direct deposited ensures that I don't get my hands on it before it lands in my savings account. For the rest of the tips in this book, I will use my "home bank," but for surefire savings, there's no better way to go than traditional.

It's easy to set up direct deposit to your savings. First, if you don't have a savings account, you'll need to open one at the bank. Tell them you're not looking for any bells and whistles, you're not looking to earn interest (you probably won't anyway), that you just need a safe place to keep your money. Then, as you're setting up the account, ask the teller to give you the paperwork required to set up direct deposit. You will more than likely have to take this paperwork to your human resources department (or whoever handles paychecks at your job) and designate a set amount to be automatically deposited.

What if you don't know how much money to set aside for your savings? The easiest way to figure out a good number is to use a percentage of your average paycheck. If you are just starting out with savings or you really need most of your take-home pay, try 5 percent. For instance, if you get paid twice monthly and each paycheck is on average about $1,200, you could designate $60 to go to your savings. If you are feeling a bit more adventurous, try

10 percent. At $1,200, that would be $120 every paycheck. You can also just choose a number that makes you comfortable, like $25 or $50. There's no right answer, just whatever works for you.

My challenge to you is when you get a pay raise, bump up the auto-deposit to your savings. Many financial gurus call it "paying yourself first." You won't be sorry that you made an investment in yourself, especially when you are able to start funding the life of your dreams.

Remember Me Not

Here's another trick to surefire savings: forget about it! Once you've handled the setup of the direct deposit, you don't have to do anything more but go to work, earn a paycheck, and allow the savings to grow on its own. There have been months when I just don't think about my savings account. I forget it's there.

Later, when I remember to go online to check the balance, I am always pleasantly surprised to see how it's grown since the last time I looked. That's the beauty of automated savings. Besides setting it up, you don't have to do anything more. And, you really won't miss the money because you'll become accustomed to living off the rest of your paycheck that doesn't go into savings.

Ready . . . Set . . . Save!

At the end of each chapter, I'll include some practical to-do's to get your savings account moving in the right direction. If you take action, you will start seeing results quicker than you could have imagined!

- If you haven't automated a portion of your paycheck to a savings account, what are you waiting for? Get thou to a bank and make it happen! Figure out a percentage of 5–10 percent of your take-home pay or a set amount (like $25 or $50) that you are comfortable with and fill out and submit the necessary paperwork to get direct deposit set up. The sooner you do it, the sooner you can sit back and watch your money grow effortlessly!

- Figure out your "magic number" or percentage that you would like to set aside from each paycheck. **Important note:** if you are married, you might want to consult your significant other and make this decision together, especially if you have a joint checking or savings account!

- Have you gotten a pay raise recently? Think about bumping up the percentage or dollar amount that gets auto-deposited into your savings. Remember, you're "paying yourself first."

Chapter 3: Creative Savings #1: Grocery Shopping Savings

The first date I went on with my now husband revealed just how differently we thought about money and savings. We began the evening by eating at a fabulous local steak-and-seafood restaurant where we held hands for the first time. Then we capped off a magical dinner with a trip to Target. It makes me laugh writing that, but back when I was first getting to know Jamie, doing anything with him was both fun and interesting, because it was with him.

He needed to pick up "a few things" for his new apartment. I didn't know how vastly different our definitions of "a few things" would be. A few things to me meant three or four items on my list, at the cheapest price I could find them. That often meant I was buying store brand. I was only earning a part-time income as a single woman and every dollar counted. So I was a little more than surprised when Jamie started shopping for a few things and ended up with a cart full of fun items I could only dream about buying.

I don't remember all of the items he dropped into the red cart, but I distinctly remember him grabbing a giant multipack of Starbucks cappuccino beverages. When we went through the checkout, he seemed surprised by the total, and I asked him, "Don't you ever look at prices?" He said "no." I also asked him if he'd ever used a shopping list or coupons and that was also a "no." In response, I said something like, "I'll teach you how."

Fast-forward eight years and we have truly become a team when it comes to grocery shopping. Every week, we keep a running list of all the items we need. We plan several dinners at home and list the ingredients. Then on Saturday, I match coupons to the items and we grocery shop together. We have both learned to compromise when it comes to spending on groceries: he sticks to the list and I don't go el-cheapo all the time.

I do sometimes use coupons, but do not have the time to spend hours each week clipping them. I used to clip the Sunday circular coupons but found it was easier to print the same coupons online. But the majority of the time, I shop the sale items and use my Target Cartwheel app to score the most savings.

Before launching into the first creative savings technique, take a moment to answer the following questions about how you shop for groceries. The answers will come in handy later in the chapter.

~~~~~

Question 1

How often do you shop for groceries? Once a day? Once a week? Whenever the fridge and pantry are empty, and you can't bring yourself to eat an expired can of Spam?

Question 2

Do you use coupons? If so, would you label yourself as a coupon fanatic or an occasional couponer?

Question 3

Do you use a store loyalty card or some other system that earns you perks for shopping at a certain place for groceries? Do you buy items when they are on sale or clearance?

~~~~~

Answer 1

Based on your answer to the first question, you can immediately begin saving money by implementing a flexible meal plan into your life. If you already do that, you are probably already on the way to maximizing your grocery savings.

If you go to the store every few days to purchase ingredients for dinner each night, you are more likely to spend more on groceries overall, because you won't think about $20 here and $30 there adding up quickly. You might also have the tendency to buy many different ingredients when you could streamline a list and buy fewer ingredients that can be used in multiple meals.

Taking a little time to decide on a few simple dinners for the week and then shopping for them in one afternoon can bring such a boost to your savings and also curtail your stress level. When your daughter tugs on your pant leg and asks you what's for dinner, you won't have to scratch your head and come up with an idea on the fly.

Ultimately, you have to do what works best for your family. But making a list for the upcoming week, planning a few weeknight dinners ahead of time, and shopping once a week will most likely give you the most bang for your buck.

Answer 2

The second question explores the use of cents-off coupons for buying specific products. This is not a book on couponing, nor am I a die-hard couponer. I use them when I have them, but I'm not obsessive. I don't often find coupons for the food we use the most: fresh, antibiotic-free, chicken breasts; colorful fruits and veggies; and gallons of milk. Coupons mostly come in handy on household items, such as paper goods, diapers and wipes, trash bags, and laundry detergent. Those are the areas where I save the most using coupons.

Answer 3

The third question deals with where you shop. Are you a person who only shops at one store each week? Or are you willing to go where the deals are and shop multiple places for sales and clearance items? If I were writing a book about getting the best deals on groceries, I might recommend shopping the sales at all your local grocery and big name stores. However, in this case, time is money and it will most definitely save you time to do all your shopping in one place. Choose the place where you most like to shop for weekly groceries and that is where you can try this savings technique.

Often, stores have loyalty cards, their own special coupons, special clearance or sales days, or some other rewards system that will help you save money when you shop there. The most important part of your shopping experience is to save your receipts. You will need them for this savings tip.

Lock in the Grocery Store Savings

I don't know about you, but I get a little thrill when I look at the bottom of my grocery store receipt and see "Total Savings Today: $X.XX." That total will reflect any coupons used, items on sale or clearance, and any store loyalty perks (like Target Cartwheel). But besides the thrill of what I did save, what is the purpose of this blurb on my receipt? The store's purpose is to get me coming back the following week because I "saved so much on my last trip." But if I'm using a debit or credit card as payment, that savings doesn't feel much different than if I hadn't saved anything. I still have to swipe a card either way.

The first creative savings tip is to stockpile your weekly grocery savings on a monthly basis. You can do this several different ways depending on how you pay, and I'll explain as we go along.

This savings technique is fairly straightforward. Keep your grocery receipt and save the money your receipt claims you saved. Do this every time you go to the store and add up your savings during the course of a month. I bet you'll be surprised how quickly it adds up!

Let's talk about a few logistical ways to accomplish this savings tip. Maybe you like to use cash when you shop for groceries. That will make this savings tip even easier to achieve. Let's say you have $130 cash to spend on groceries for the week. Your grand total comes out $115. You pay cash and have $15 left over. But the bottom of your receipt claims you saved $7.55 (includes coupons, sales, and clearance pricing). Round up that total to $8 and put aside that cash when you get home.

Remember that savings envelope we talked about at the beginning of this book? That would be a great place to keep your grocery store savings. Roll over the remaining $7 to next week's grocery cash. And, next week, repeat the same process again, pulling out the cash you "saved" as indicated at the bottom of the receipt.

What if you don't use cash, but prefer to use your debit card? You can still follow the same process as above with a tweak. Look at your receipt to determine the dollar amount that you saved and, as soon as possible, transfer that amount from your checking account to your savings account. This is especially easy if you have your checking and savings accounts linked. You can simply do a quick online transfer from the comfort of your own home.

Or perhaps, you're like me and want to really feel your money, but you don't shop with cash at the grocery store. Use your debit card as normal, but make sure you save your grocery store receipts for several weeks. In fact, if you decide to use this method, it will be best to save your receipts until the end of the month.

Add up your total savings, and then withdraw that amount and put it in your envelope or your savings box. For example: you compile all your grocery receipts for one month and, at the end of the month, you have the following totals: $8.55, $12.30, $4.29, and $10.70. The total you saved for the month on groceries is $35.84. Obviously, you can't go to the ATM and withdrawal this exact amount. But you can round up (you're not really going to miss that extra $5, right?) and withdraw $40 for savings. And, just like that, you're turning your savings on groceries into actual cash money.

It goes without saying that the more you save at the store, the more you will be able to put into your savings account with this tip. However, even if you start small and save only $20 or so, it's more money in your savings, and it will add up over time! If you're on the other end of the spectrum and consider yourself an extreme couponer, using this tip alone could fund part of your summer vacation in a few months!

The important thing is to go at a pace that is comfortable for you, shop for your groceries as close to once a week as possible, and start stockpiling your store savings!

How It Worked for Me

The first week, my grocery store savings was low, because I sent my husband while I took my son on an outing and also because I didn't prepare coupons for any of our items. So our grocery store savings came solely from the in-store sales that particular Saturday. The savings was $8.74.

The next week, Jamie amped up our savings by using a high-value coupon for our favorite, brand-name contact solution and by using the Target Cartwheel app on most of our other groceries. This time, our savings kicked up to $13.70! We haven't finished the month yet, but I know we will have saved at least $22. I'm challenging myself to double that and deposit $45 into our savings by the end of the month.

Ready . . . Set . . . Save

- The key to this savings tip is to shop often enough that you can stockpile some cash savings during the month. So consider keeping an on-going list of grocery items you need throughout the week and choose a day each week to do your shopping. I recommend Saturday or Sunday because you can prepare meal ideas and your list of ingredients for the upcoming week. You can wait until the weekly circular comes out and make a list based on sale items.

- Figure out which version of this savings tip you will use. Will you spend cash at the store and immediately set aside your savings? Will you swipe a card and have your savings deposited to your account? Will you use your card and withdraw your rounded-up savings at the end of the month from an ATM? Maybe you can think of a way not listed here that would work even better for you. It doesn't really matter as long as you make it your own and go out there and save some cash!

- If you are using the once-a-month withdrawal method, be sure to save your receipts so you can add up your total store savings. If you don't want to save them, be sure to write down your totals each week, preferably on the same piece of paper!

Chapter 4: Creative Savings #2: Habit Building and Savings

I signed up for this eight-week health challenge with some ladies at my church. The premise is simple. Every single day for eight weeks, I earn points for categories like eating two servings of fruit, three servings of vegetables, drinking 64 ounces of water, and not eating sweets. At the end of each week, I tally up my points, plus any added points for pounds lost and then report it to the team. I compete against the other ladies and at the end of the eight weeks, the person who has lost the most weight splits the pay-in fee ($20 per participant) with the person who has earned the most points overall.

I don't know what I was thinking when I signed up for this challenge. I must have gone temporarily out of my head, because I actually thought to myself, "This will be easy. I've got this in the bag." In reality, less than a week into it, I bemoaned the fact that I couldn't have chocolate every day as I normally do!

The ladies participating have our own private message board where we report our points and encourage one another. One day, a woman shared her secret for getting in the required weekly workouts. She has a clear jar and every time she completes a workout, she drops a dollar into the jar. At the end of the challenge, she plans on buying herself something fun.

When I read her idea, it motivated me. I love the idea of exercising and putting a little cash aside as a reward. If this will work successfully for exercise, I propose that it will work for any positive habit you or I might be trying to establish in our lives.

To Establish a New Habit, Pay Yourself

It's extremely motivating to watch a jar fill up with cash while my pants get looser and my arms get more toned! It seems like a no-brainer to work on establishing one good habit and all the while I'm also working on my savings habit. If you think this sounds like an easy way to save, why not give it a try and see how much money you can rack up by the end of the month.

How will you decide which habit to "compensate" yourself for? The next time you get a chance to have a little quiet time (for some of us, that's in short supply!), stop and really think about an area where you'd like to see improvement in your life. Maybe you're like my friend and you need the extra motivation to get off the couch and move. Maybe you feel that your family eats too many meals out and you'd like to cook at home more often. Or you want your home to stay tidy during the week, but you're having trouble remembering to clean up each day before you collapse exhaustedly into bed (true story!). Maybe you want to become a better reader, but never give yourself quality time to actually sit down with a cup of coffee and a book.

The truth is, there will always be positive habits we long to cultivate in our own lives. We will never arrive at perfection. So the hardest choice will probably be choosing a habit. Just remember that this is your life and your savings you're trying to improve on. You can always change it up once you get into the habit of doing something. When that habit is established, you can move on to something else and pay yourself for that.

What's it going to be? Did you choose a habit yet? Ok, now let's talk about your rate of pay.

Setting Your Quantity Rate

This savings tip is all about *quantity,* meaning the more you practice it, the more you "pay" yourself, hence the more you save. Although quality is important, we're not as concerned about it now since we are trying to simultaneously establish a good habit and save some green. Quality will naturally improve as you get better and more automatic at your habit.

You need to decide what you want your rate of pay to be. Are you good with a dollar? If that sounds too steep or you're going to be practicing your habit multiple times per day, like drinking eight ounces of water, maybe you should start with something smaller, such as a quarter. Or it could be the opposite. You might feel like pumping up your savings and pledge $5 every time you practice your habit. It doesn't really matter as long as you choose an amount that will be motivating to you.

Now you have the habit that you want to work on and you've decided on your rate of pay. Time to put this savings tip into action.

You'll need a piece of paper. If you're anything like me, this won't be a problem since you hoard countless pretty papers just waiting to be used in your craft closet. Come on, I know I'm not the only one!

Honestly, it really doesn't matter what you use as long as you do this exercise. You've got to make it real and you've got to commit to your good habit and savings goal by writing it down.

Using the writing utensil of your choice, write out the following statement and fill in the blanks.

**For (time limit), I will pay myself (rate of pay in $$)
each time I (good habit I'm trying to cultivate).**

B. Franklin

Then, somewhere nearby, sign your name. I guess you don't really have to sign your name, but somehow that seems to make it more official, don't you think?

Let me give you some examples:

**For the entire month of May,
I will pay myself $1
each time I log a writing session of at least ten
minutes or more.**

~~~~~

**For the next two weeks,
I will pay myself $.25
each time I drink eight ounces of water.**

~~~~~

**For the entire month of July,
I will pay myself $2
each time I cook a meal at home instead of drive-
through a fast-food restaurant.**

~~~~

See how easy that is? Once you've figured out exactly what you want to do, just personalize it, and you're ready to begin. Once you've written your goal down, you've got to find a prominent home for you new "artwork" for the length of time you'll be working on your goal.

Put it somewhere you will see it! Here's why. If you tuck the paper away somewhere, you'll go about your life as normal. You'll probably even log a couple of triumphs at practicing your new positive goal. But, you might be in the moment and not have time to grab the money you promised yourself and more than likely, you'll forget to pay yourself your fee. If you have that paper in a prominent place, it's not only going to remind you to practice your goal, but also to pay yourself. It's a win-win all around!

The Practical Stuff

You'll need a place to stash your growing supply of cash. I recommend a clear jar with a lid. You want to be able to see the jar filling up as time passes. Again, this will serve as a visual reminder that not only is your savings growing, but you're also practicing your positive habit regularly.

You can get a glass jar at most discount stores or grocery stores for less than $10. Maybe you already have one at home. I do recommend using one with a lid that can be screwed on tightly. Otherwise, other members of your household might accidentally mistake your magic jar of money for a "help yourself to this growing pile of cash" fund!

It's a good idea to tell your family what you are doing. You can even label the jar with "Savings for Our Vacation" or whatever your savings goal is. That will serve as a reminder to everyone who sees the jar that it's not a free-for-all.

Put the jar where you'll see it, just like the paper you wrote earlier to get you started with this savings tip. The more you see it, the more inspired you'll be to get to work on your habit and fill the jar up!

Obviously, you're going to need a supply of either coins or green money in order to pull this savings tip off. Someone might suggest using something non-monetary (like colored marbles) that represent cash and exchanging it out for the real thing later on, but I don't see this as being very successful. I am not motivated by pebbles or marbles; they don't mean much to me. That's why I say, stick with cash or coins if you can. After all, your ultimate goal is to save more money, so you're going to have to have some in the first place.

So, yes, this saving habit is going to require you to visit the ATM or bank. But it doesn't have to be a financial stress on your budget. Just choose a category for the month that you are comfortable paying cash for. For my family, this category would be our extra spending money, or "mad money" as we like to call it. For all of us, it's about $40 in cash a week.

So I would get that out and spend it like usual, but tuck a few dollars away for the specific purpose of throwing them in the jar when I practice my habit. If you're saving change, you can do the same thing. Spend as normal, but keep your change, especially the denomination that you're dropping into the jar. You won't need to remove any more money from your bank account than you normally would as long as you stay on budget for the category you're using cash for.

Add Up the Positive

Here's another neat idea you might want to try while practicing this savings tip. There's a cool concept called "habit-stacking." I learned about this from S. J. Scott's book, _Habit Stacking: 97 Small Life Changes That Take Five Minutes or Less_, and I highly recommend reading it! The idea behind habit stacking is to take several good habits that take minutes to accomplish, group them together, and practice them all at one time each day. When you get into the habit of doing these things together, you are injecting a whole lot of discipline into your life, but not taking a whole lot of time. I practice habit stacking most frequently in the morning to help streamline my morning routine.

Here's my morning habit stack in the order I do it:

- Eat breakfast.

- Drink eight ounces of ice water.

- Take my multivitamin.

- Read my devotional for the day.

- Make the bed.

- Pick up five things and return them to their "home."

- Write down my top three priorities to accomplish for the day.

Notice that all these actions are positive, and none of them take any more than five minutes to accomplish. In fact, most of the time, I can complete the whole cycle in fifteen minutes or less. I could easily adapt this habit-stacking procedure to my savings tip and pay myself each time I complete the cycle.

If you decide you want to try this, first choose five to seven quick habits you'd like to stack. Then arrange them by the most logical order (group them according to what rooms you'll need to be in, for example). Decide what time of day you will practice these habits. Finally, complete the writing exercise at the beginning of the chapter and set your rate of pay. Make sure you complete the whole cycle of habits or you don't get paid! Also, try to complete your habit stacking at the same time each day so it becomes even more automatic.

Habit stacking is a quick way to build a series of good habits, making them almost automatic, and it also helps you with your savings goals. I hope you'll give it a try!

How It Worked for Me

I decided to choose two positive habits to work on while practicing this particular savings tip. Because I need to get more consistent exercise each week, I pledged to pay myself $1 each time I exercised for thirty minutes or longer. Also, for the month, every time I logged a writing session, I also paid myself $1. At the end of the month (May, in this case), all the money I stockpiled was funneled into my savings for my New York trip (only a month away)!

Ready . . . Set . . . Save

- Decide which positive habit you'd like to work on for a set amount of time, such as a month or six weeks. Then decide on your rate of pay that you will put away each time you practice your habit. On a sheet of paper, write out your pledge:

For (time limit),
I will pay myself (rate of pay in $$)
each time I (good habit I'm trying to cultivate).

- Choose a see-through jar so you can watch your savings build as you practice your positive habit. This will serve as motivation for you to keep going, especially when you're tired or lacking willpower. Just think of how your savings will benefit while you're in the process of improving your life!

- Got too many positive habits you want to work on at once? Not a problem! Try habit stacking: grouping several quick habits together and practicing them in succession. Figure out the most logical order to perform them, write down your sequence, and decide on a time of day you will use your habit-stacking technique. And don't forget to set your rate

of pay and pay yourself when you complete the
sequence!

Bonus Chapter:
8 Ways to Save and Get Fit

Let's face it: your health is everything. You could have all the money in the world to do anything you want to do and not be able to do it because of poor health. Or, maybe you're just getting started on this savings journey and don't see how you'll be able to fit in health and wellness without shelling out major bucks for an expensive gym membership and personal trainer.

I'm here to tell you that not only is it possible to get fit for practically nothing, but people all over the world are practicing these creative tips that save money and help them shape up!

- **Try a fitness DVD.** Do you have a favorite celebrity trainer? Great! Consider that person your new personal trainer and purchase one of his/her fitness DVDs. Many trainers include a structured plan that will tell you how many days a week to work out to the DVD. Some DVDs even include a free trial to the trainer's website. You can try a more in-depth plan online; just don't forget to cancel when the trial is up!

- **Find an inexpensive gym.** You can often find, in many US cities, a gym in your area for about $10 a month. Obviously, a gym this cheap won't have many frills, but you can't go wrong with free weights, cardio machines, and balance balls! If you're unsure how to use the equipment, just ask one of the gym workers.

- **Take your routine outdoors.** This one is a no-brainer for me because I live in Florida, where the weather stays mild most of the year. Wherever you live, capitalize on the nice seasons, like spring and fall, and take your exercise outdoors. Walk, jog, ride a bike; you can even take your yoga mat outside and practice on a flat surface. Not only will you get a great workout, but you'll also get the benefit of fresh air and feel even more energized after your workout.

- **Take your routine indoors.** To the mall, that is! When the weather is less than desirable for outside exercise, plan to do some cardio walking at the mall. Here's the catch: leave your purse or your wallet securely locked in the trunk of your car so even if you're tempted to stop and shop, you can't.

- **There's an app for that!** Chances are, whatever exercise you're most interested in has multiple apps available to help you become a pro. Several weeks ago, I searched for yoga apps, read a few reviews online, and bought one I liked for $3.99. I have used the app about twenty times and already love the results I'm seeing from it.

- **There's probably a book for that too!** We're such a technology-driven culture these days that we tend to forget that books still make fabulous resources. There's no need to pay for them either when you probably have a public library nearby. Your library is sure to have several books about home fitness that will interest you. The best part is that you can gain more knowledge about fitness for free with a swipe of your library card.

- **Split a personal trainer, or marry one.** I joke about the second part because my husband loves to work out and used to be a personal trainer. Hence, he makes a great resource for me when I need to know the correct form and correct way to perform any given exercise. But, if you don't happen to be married to a trainer, you could find a few friends who were interested in a personal trainer and go in together on the cost. Many trainers will offer cheaper rates for groups than single training sessions.

- **Try house walking.** Unlike sleepwalking, house walking does actually require you to be awake. House walking can be as simple as taking a lap around your home during a television show commercial break or pacing the living room while you're on a phone call. Use your creativity to come up with ways to keep moving in your own home instead of becoming a couch potato. You'll get in better shape and have more energy too.

Chapter 5: Creative Savings #3: Piggy Bank Party!

Much of what I know about saving money, I learned from my awesome and frugal mama. After I was born, she had the great privilege of being a stay-at-home mom, one of the most underrated, unappreciated jobs, in my opinion. I'm proud of the fact that my dad was willing to work extra hours to provide for our family so mom could be at every school event, every doctor's appointment, and every performance or game my sister and I had. I love that my mom was willing to sacrifice having a life of her own to be there for us without fail when we needed her. As a result, she became quite the home economist. She used coupons often, and found amazing bargains on clearance. She also was the one who demonstrated this savings tip for me.

Mom had a lovely clear, glass piggy bank that didn't have a stopper at the bottom. When she was ready to take her coins out, she had to turn it upside down over a towel and use a butter knife to jimmy the coins out, a few at a time. Of course, this was great fun for us kids when Mom got out her piggy bank, because it meant someone was getting a present.

My dad, my sister, and I all have birthdays that are spread out throughout the year, so my mom would always save her nickels, dimes, and quarters and put them in the glass pig. Any time one of us had a birthday coming up, she would shake all the change out of the pig, which was usually filled to the top at that point and use the money to spend on the closest birthday coming up. She also taught us how to sort the coins and wrap them up perfectly in the coin wrappers.

I don't remember if it was when I moved several states away or when I got married, but my mom eventually gave me that bank. Every time I see it, I am reminded of those sweet memories of filling it up with coins in anticipation of an upcoming birthday.

Fill 'er Up!

Piggy banks seem to be in vogue these days. Only, you can find so much more than pigs made into banks. You can probably find a bank in just about any conceivable character, shape or size. I actually have three in my house right now: the glass one from my mom, a cute black-and-white, polka-dot pig, and a baby blue pig that says "Little Prince" on the side. The last one is what I'm currently using because it belongs to my son. I want to pass along this coin savings tip to him.

If you have a coin bank of any kind, you are ready to begin this savings tip. This is one that you can easily use while you are working through the other tips in the book. The bank gives you a place for your change if you're not sure what to do with it.

This is also a tip to get the whole family involved in. You'll want to place the pig somewhere common to everyone, such as a living room shelf (but out of reach of little ones if your bank is breakable) and let them know that for the next month, or whatever length of time you set, everyone can throw their change in the piggy bank.

You can decide if you want to include pennies along with the silver coins, but I recommend just putting silver coins in the bank since they are of higher denominations. You could also designate a separate jar or bank for all the pennies. This makes it easier when it's time to sort and wrap your coins and teaches your little ones how to sort by color!

No Extra Cash Required

Like the previous savings tip, you don't really need to earn extra cash to make this work. You just need to use cash money and hang on to your change. I don't know about you, but when I have cash to spend, it is not difficult for me to acquire plenty of change by the end of the day! Right now, my husband and I are on a business trip in Nashville, Tennessee, and we brought along cash for our spending money. At the end of each day, we've been gathering our coins on the hotel desk, and I suspect that by the end of our trip, we'll have quite a lot to take back to Florida. All of the silver coins will go in my son's piggy bank. I have a separate place for the pennies.

All you really need to get started is a piggy bank (of some sort) and some coins. You'll need to decide if you're going to save them for a specific length of time before wrapping them or if you just want to keep packing the bank with coins until it's full. The more you put in, the higher your total will be, but you'd be surprised at how quickly you can create a stockpile of coins and save $30, $40, or $50 in no time at all.

Piggy Party

It can get a little tedious when it's time to dump your coins, sort them, and wrap them up so you can exchange them for paper money. That's where the idea for a Piggy Party comes in. Why not make your coin savings a celebration for the whole family? You'll be instilling basic savings skills in your kids and sharpening their math skills.

When you're ready to wrap your coins, plan a time to perform the activity, allowing at least an hour, especially if your kids will be doing it for the first time. You could even plan your Piggy Party as an evening activity and serve themed foods for dinner. (Pigs in a blanket, anyone?)

Place a towel on the surface where you will empty your coins from the piggy bank. You don't want the change to go every which way and bounce all over the floor. Show your children how to empty the bank and proceed to empty the entire bank before beginning to wrap your coins.

Next, divide the silver coins into three different categories: dimes, nickels, and quarters. If any pennies accidentally made it into the bank, you'll want to separate those out so they don't mistakenly end up being wrapped with the silver coins. Once all the coins have been categorized, you're ready to start wrapping them.

Below are how many coins you need in each category to fill a coin wrapper:

- **Nickels**: You need 40 nickels to make a $2 roll. Make piles of 5 nickels each. Once you have eight piles, you have enough for a roll.

- **Dimes**: You need 50 dimes to make a $5 roll. Make piles of 10 dimes each. Once you have five piles, you have enough for a roll.

- **Quarters**: You need 40 quarters to make a $10 roll. Make piles of 4 quarters each. Once you have ten piles, you have enough for a roll.

- **Pennies**: (just in case) You need 50 pennies to make a $.50 roll. Make piles of 10 pennies each. Once you have five piles, you have enough for a roll.

Even if you just ended up with one roll of each kind of silver coin, you would still come away with $17! That's not bad for using a saving's tip with minimum effort! Just imagine what you could save if you filled the bank to the top before wrapping your coins.

Where To Now?

After you've had your Piggy Party, wrapped your coins, and hopefully had a fun evening of learning and laughter, it's time to take your coins to the bank. Literally.

There are kiosks at many grocery stores that will take your unwrapped coins, but many of them charge a fee and some won't give you cash back, exchanging your coins for gift cards instead. I suppose that will work fine if you want to shop at a certain place, but this is a book on saving, not spending. You're putting aside your coins so you can save more money.

In this case, it's best to take your wrapped coins straight to your bank. Make sure it's a bank of which you are a member; many banks won't exchange your coins for cash unless you already have an account with them. It used to be that in order to exchange your coins, you had to write your account number on the side of the wrapper. The last time I asked if I needed to do this, the teller said it wasn't necessary and even a little dangerous to have my account number floating around on my coin wrappers.

If you have questions about your own bank's procedures for taking coins, it's a good idea to call them before making the trip. The bank might even offer to take your unwrapped coins and sort them with its coin-counting machine. Be sure to check, if you'd like them to do the work for you. But it's not nearly as fun as the Piggy Party!

One other note: please don't try to go through the bank drive through to drop off your coins! First, they probably won't fit in the little tube that gets sucked up and whisked away to the teller. Second, they will probably be too heavy to get sucked up. And finally, this is just one of those things you'll need to use face-to-face interaction to accomplish. Be genuinely kind to the teller and I'm sure he or she will return the favor and be happy to exchange your wrapped coins for bills.

How It Worked for Me

I love this savings tip because it's one of the easiest "no brainers" presented in the book; not to mention, I've been saving coins in this manner most of my life. But writing this chapter helped me to focus even more on stockpiling my coins for the purpose of putting them in my son's piggy bank.

Yesterday, I pulled out my wallet, which had a lot of extra change in it from a trip I'd just returned from. I made a big deal to my twenty-month-old son about getting his blue piggy bank off the high shelf in his room and showing him how to "feed" it. Of course, I supervised the entire time to make sure none of the silver coins went into his mouth, but he seemed to greatly enjoy putting the coins in the pig. And the process is helping him with his fine motor skills. Even though he doesn't understand what he is doing, I am laying the foundation of a simple savings habit that I hope he'll use all his life.

Ready . . . Set . . . Save

- If you don't own a coin bank of some sort, what are you waiting for? Pick your favorite character or animal and there's probably a coin bank that looks like it. Or, if you're not picky, head to the nearest discount store and pick up an old-fashioned piggy bank. That's all you need to get started saving your coins!

- Be sure to let everyone in the family know about the coin bank and place it in a central location so it's easily accessible (except to the little ones!). Decide if you will only collect silver coins or also include pennies. Decide if you will save your coins for a certain length of time or until the bank is full.

- Don't forget coin wrappers! They're inexpensive and can be found at drug and discount stores, usually with the office supplies. You can ask your bank, and they might give the wrappers to you. Make sure you have enough of each kind of wrapper before having your Piggy Party.

Chapter 6: Creative Savings #4: Percentage Savings Plan

There is a great book by successful speaker and businessman Brian Tracy titled _No Excuses: The Power of Self-Discipline._ I recently finished reading it after picking it up on clearance at Barnes and Noble, and I truly believe it has the information in it to double my income. I don't know if I can say that about many books, but this one has so much great stuff in it, I'll probably have to read it several times just to begin to absorb and apply the information.

One of the chapters in the book relates personal finance to self-discipline. Tracy states that it takes extreme self-discipline to be able to manage your finances throughout your life and become a wealthy person. Most of us don't possess the self-discipline to live beneath our means. As soon as we get a raise, we adjust the level of our living expenses to meet it, so we never end up putting any money back.

I wrote this book to give you hope that even if you are on a tight budget or have a low income, you *can* make the choice to hold back money for your future dreams and goals, even if you have to do it in creative ways. You *can* make the choice today to live beneath your means, so later on you can experience the realization of having more than enough. But it is a choice. And you will have to decide if it's a choice worth making in your life.

Have you ever thought about the fact that, in most situations, we already know exactly what to do, but, for whatever reason, we don't take the time or expend the energy to do what is necessary? Just this past week, I dealt with a situation that has been going on for months, and, deep down inside, I've always known what I needed to do (confront the issue head-on with the person causing it); yet I've dragged my feet about taking action. Finally, I scheduled a day and time to deal with it and even built in some accountability measures so I followed through. How much time and energy would have been saved if I'd just dealt with it in the beginning? The answer in this case is months!

That's the way many of us are with our money. You get an extra check here or there. Maybe an unexpected birthday gift or inheritance comes through. You know deep down that you need to be responsible for the extra cash to really make it work for your benefit, but instead you just let it sit in your bank account while you enjoy looking at the hefty balance of your account.

What happens two months down the road? Because, I'm sorry, money never just sits in a bank account! It's going to go somewhere. One day you're going to look at that account and think, "Where did the extra money go?" Life happened, and because you weren't proactive with the extra money in the beginning, it quietly slipped away as money so often does.

This savings tip is all about being proactive with your money. You have to decide once and for all that you will be in charge of the money that comes through your hands (which is quite a lot, if you add it up over a lifetime) and will have something to show for it in the form of savings.

Start Small

I get it that there are so many people struggling to make ends meet in our country and in the world today. So many people live paycheck to paycheck. That's the reason many say they think that they can never get ahead with savings and money because they don't have enough to begin with. If you are one of those people whose family is struggling, I'm here to tell you that there is hope! And even if you can only afford to put away coins for savings right now (see the previous chapter), small beginnings count and they do add up over time.

You can put back a little here and there and watch your savings grow to unbelievable heights. I'm not even talking about interest, which is nearly non-existent on savings accounts these days. I'm talking about the act of you telling your money where to go and then putting it there. Even tiny crumbs will start to build up on the floor if they're not swept up from time to time.

For this savings tip, I am asking you to immediately save 1 percent of your take-home pay. You are going to adjust your lifestyle to live on 99 percent of your take-home pay with the other 1 percent going to savings. Once you get acclimated to living on 99 percent of your income, you will adjust your lifestyle to live on 98 percent. And so on and so forth until you have reached living on 90 percent of your take-home pay with 10 percent going into savings. Note that this savings is meant be used on top of the automated savings we talked about in Chapter 2 of this book. The rest of your pay that you receive after the automated amount is considered 100 percent of your take-home pay.

Let's look at the numbers to see how doable this really is. Let's say your household income per month is $4,200 after taxes (I am basing this on the median American family income of roughly $55,000 a year). In order to work this savings tip, you would need to adjust your lifestyle to live on $4,158 each month, instead of the full $4,200. One percent of $4,200 is $42 and that will go immediately to your savings. You can either allocate it there or have it put there via direct deposit. In a few months, once you get used to living on $42 less per month, give yourself a "pay raise" and change your savings to two percent or $84. Once again, you will have to adjust your lifestyle, but only by $42 because you've already been used to living on 1 percent less than your total take-home pay.

This savings tip is really going to work wonders for your life if you'll try it. First, you are taking mere "crumbs" from your income and piling them up. You are paying yourself first, and although you are starting out small, those small amounts will add up faster than you can imagine. Second, you are practicing a valuable habit that will serve you the rest of your life if you will keep it up: living on less than you make. If you ask most millionaires what the key to becoming rich is, they will tell you it is a lot of hard work over time while living beneath your means!

Can you imagine how the economic face of America would change, seemingly overnight, if the majority of working Americans put away 1–10 percent of their income into savings? I don't think we can imagine how quickly economic hardship would diminish.

Instead it seems our country is headed toward even more fiscal debt. The government is trillions of dollars in debt, and the economy tries to sell us the lie that credit is the answer to all our problems. Don't have the cash? No problem! Just pull out your plastic and worry about where the money is going to come from later. Only, what happens when "later" comes and you still don't have the money? You're stuck with the debt and an astronomical interest rate, compounded on top of that.

No, I propose there is a better way. Pay cash, eliminate debt, and save a little bit of your income. This habit is slowly changing my life and the lives of my immediate family members. And it starts with just a tiny 1 percent.

The "B" Word

I'm going to use a word that might cause you to toss down this book or the electronic device you're reading it on and run from the room screaming! You see, if you are going to make this savings tip work, you are going to have to employ a non-creative solution, but a necessary one, and that is a budget. There, I said it. Have you calmed down yet? Ok. Read on, friend.

The only way you can make your money work for you and ensure you are actually setting aside the right amount of your take-home pay is to know where all your money is going in the first place. You have to have a plan. And that plan is known as the budget.

I'm not going to go into a detailed description of what your budget should look like. Not only is that outside the scope of this book, but you can also find many amazing resources about how to make the most effective budget for you. A budget needs to be personalized for your family and its needs. In fact, no two budgets should ever look alike. We all have different salaries and paychecks and even those can vary from month to month.

You should do a budget for 100 percent of your household income at the beginning of the month. You will forecast where 99 percent of your money will go and include the remaining 1 percent in the savings category, if you're just starting this savings tip. Complete a new budget for each month and as you go along, find the areas of fixed expenses (staying the same) and variable expenses (changing) that you might be able to lower in order to raise your rate of savings pay to 2 percent.

This is where the power of the budget really comes in handy. If you can see where your money is going ahead of time, you can always decide to allocate it differently in order to squeeze some extra money into savings. Not to mention, once you budget long enough, you'll get better and better at dictating the direction of your money and growing fiscally responsible. If you have a hard month, you can tighten the reins as needed, knowing that it's only a month and finances can often change on a dime (no pun intended). Most likely, next month will be better.

As you work through the budgeting process, you can decide how quickly you want to increase your percentage of savings until you hit the 10 percent mark. Once you've reached this point, you'll have quite a bit of savings in the bank and might be ready to start paying it out on those dream goals you defined at the beginning of the book.

Going back to our previous example: if your household income is $4,200 per month and you've been budgeting and saving for a while, you'll already have some money in the bank. But now, let's say you're up to the 10 percent goal of savings and you do this for a year. Ten percent of $4,200 is $420. If you save this every month from January to December, by the end of the year, you'll have $5,040 in savings, not including the money you saved at 1, 2, 3, 4, 5, 6, 7, 8, and 9 percent of your take-home pay! That's some serious cash!

There's Always Hope

I think this chapter has the potential to be one of the most empowering chapters in the book, simply because it shows you that even as little as 1 percent of your income can help you start to realize your savings goals in time. Holding a little bit of your money back can empower you to see that you are worth investing in, first and foremost.

I hope this chapter has provided encouragement for anyone who is struggling to make ends meet and just wants to jump-start his or her savings. Even if you've made disastrous decisions with your money in the past, tomorrow is a new day and you can make a different choice. You can tell your money where it will go from now on and for the rest of your life, if you so choose. You can set aside a small portion of your income and watch your savings grow and fund your dream life. It's all possible. There is always hope!

How It Worked for Me

For me, this habit hinges on being able to budget how much of a percentage I'm going to allocate to savings per month. I'm going to admit something here: I do not enjoy making a budget. Not even a little bit! But, I do enjoy telling my money where it will go before it even hits my checking account. I like knowing whether or not I'm going to have wiggle room in the month. Those are two reasons that I resolved to do a budget for each month this year. I am certain that by the time December rolls around, I'll be so used to making the monthly budget that it will be a habit I carry into the next year and beyond.

I decided to start with the 1 percent, because that's what I outline to begin with this habit. When I went to make my June budget, I allocated $50 to savings, thus leaving 99 percent of my family's take-home pay to the remainder of the budget. I plan to keep this percentage up through the end of the year and bump it up to 2 percent at the start of the new year. So far, we are right on track.

Ready . . . Set . . . Save

- Figure out what percentage of income you would like to save each month. There's no rule that says it has to start with 1 percent; that's just a jumping-off point for those who want to get their feet wet. Maybe your family is able to start off saving 5 percent. Go with what feels best for you and your family. Just put *something* aside!

- If you don't already write a monthly budget, it's time to start! A quick search on the Internet will yield thousands of options for monthly budget forms. You might choose to complete your budget entirely online or maybe you like having a hard copy, in which case, you can print out a blank form each month. If you're someone who is on your smart phone or tablet all day, research and choose a budget app. With all the options available, there is really no excuse for anyone not to have a monthly budget. If you're like me and don't enjoy doing a budget, schedule a day and time at the beginning of each month to sit down and get it done. I promise you'll feel better after you do!

- Can't seem to find the money to set aside for savings? Have an honest conversation with yourself and/or your significant other. Are you living a lifestyle that is beyond your means? Do you have hundreds of cable channels that you don't need? Do you need to champion for a pay raise at work (if you deserve one)? Do you eat out every meal instead of cooking budget-friendly meals at home? Sometimes it takes being brutally honest with yourself and your family about what you are spending (or wasting) your money on, but the truth is, there is probably always something you can do less of in order to contribute more to your savings. A little sacrifice now will bring a lot of pleasure down the road when you are reaping the benefits of good saving habits.

Chapter 7: Creative Savings #5: Christmas in June Savings!

Dave Ramsey is one of my favorite financial gurus, not only because he's so wise about money, but also because he's funny and sarcastic. One of my favorite quotes from him is,

"By the way, they've decided that Christmas is going to be on December 25th this year. You've been forewarned."

It's something to that effect. It makes me laugh because like so many others, I too am guilty of letting Christmas sneak up on me year after year, as if the date has changed, and I'm once again scrounging around for cash to buy my family and friends presents.

Last year, Black Friday rolled around and I was seriously sorry that I had let the holiday season once again sneak up on me. Had I followed the savings tip I'm about to outline, I would have had some cash to spend to get a jumpstart on my gift shopping.

How do you pay for your Christmas purchases (or Hanukkah or Kwanzaa or your specific tradition)? Are you like many Americans who put their purchases on plastic? A recent study of American spending showed that "close to half of Americans have more credit card debt than savings" (cbsnews.com, February 18, 2014). And many of those people don't have the funds to clear that debt, so they resort to monthly payments with astronomical interest rates.

So that present you bought your brother-in-law for the bargain price of $29.99 and put on your credit card? If you didn't pay it off the next month, it's a lot more expensive in the end after you tack on 24 percent interest and penalties for paying late.

Before you jump to the conclusion that I am anti-credit card, let me clear the air and tell you that I do, in fact, have a credit card. One credit card, not multiple ones. I only use it for purchases that need a credit card, such as hotels or car rentals or in a pinch if I'm traveling. And I pay the total amount due every month. I don't necessarily have a problem with having a credit card, but I do have a problem with carrying a balance (I don't) and I *refuse* to pay interest. The credit card companies would not view me as a valuable customer because I don't make them much money.

Some people do not possess the willpower to use a credit card and pay it off every month. If this is you, I am in no way getting onto you for this. Those clever credit card companies want you to only make the minimum payment or "forget" to make a payment. They make their money in payments and interest. So, if you are someone who gets into trouble when you use a credit card, it is ok. You're going to have to outsmart the credit card companies by not using a credit card! Cut it up, freeze it in water, hide it, or whatever else you have to do, but don't let the credit card companies win!

Typically, when I'm shopping for Christmas gifts, I use my debit card. I do not go into January owing anything on a credit card, so I very rarely use one for gift purchases.

While there is nothing wrong with using a debit card for gift purchases, it does have a big disadvantage.

Let's say you buy Uncle Bob a sweater from his favorite department store using your debit card. Only it turns out, the sweater is a size too small and, really, Uncle Bob doesn't actually care for that department store at all. You provide him with the receipt and he goes to the store to "exchange" the item.

But it's January and all the clothes are picked over and there's no identical sweater in his size and nothing else that he wants. So he just asks the store for a refund. Most store policies will only refund to the same method of payment on the receipt (in this case a debit card). The alternative is a store credit or gift card. Unfortunately,

Uncle Bob is now stuck with a gift card to a store he doesn't really like.

Whereas, if you had used cash and that was listed as the form of payment on the receipt, the store would most likely refund Uncle Bob the cash that he can spend anywhere on anything!

Now you know why I advocate saving up some actual cash money for your holiday shopping. Not only will you be more likely to stick to your budget (it's painful to hand those bills off!), but you'll also make any returns a whole lot easier on your family and friends.

Start Now

This savings tip is a little different from the others because it covers saving for a specific goal: holiday gift shopping. This goal will also take a little longer to get results, so you will probably want to practice it while you're working on your other savings goals. But I can guarantee that if you'll try out this tip, you'll eliminate a lot of holiday spending stress and have a pile of cash to pay for your gifts.

It is the perfect time for me to write this chapter because it's the end of May and this particular habit begins in June. Here is the game plan: by Black Friday (end of November), I would like to have $300 in cash saved up to jumpstart my Christmas shopping. By taking that amount and dividing it by the number of months I have to save (June to November is six months), I get a monthly saving's goal of $50.

Sometime during the thirty days of June, I need to come up with $50 cash money to set aside for Christmas. Once I've got my $50, I've met my goal for the month and can move on to save for other things. Then, I repeat the process for July, August, September, October, and November. When Black Friday rolls around, I'll be ready to snag some of the great deals with the cash I've been stockpiling for the past six months. But the most important part is that I need to start now! If I don't start planning ahead, the holidays will once again sneak up on me and I'll be disappointed that I don't have extra cash to spend.

There are many different ways you can easily come up with $50 extra each month. Remember, the title of this book is *8 (Really Creative) Ways to Save.* Now would be a great time to employ your creativity. Where you get the money is up to you. What kind of hobbies do you do that could potentially earn you $50? We're not talking a small business here; but maybe it's something you can do a few hours each week that quickly piles up the bucks.

I know many women who clean houses, and consequently many women who would like to hire someone to clean their houses! If you are handy with cleaning, you could clean one house and easily earn $50, if not more! Maybe you're great at organizing and can help friends or acquaintances organize their bedroom, office, or closet. You could walk dogs, babysit, cook meals, bake birthday cakes in just a few hours a week and earn $50 and more. Take your strengths and put them to work for you. There is always money to be found for the person who is willing to work.

My monthly $50 is going to come from my music studio business. The month of June is when piano and voice lessons really pick up for me, so I'm going to set aside $50 of my earnings right off the top and then I'll be done for the month. Then when July rolls along, I'll do the same thing.

Remember reading about budgeting in the last chapter? If you would prefer, you can always create a savings category for holiday gifts in your budget and allocate $50 to it each month for the next six months. You'll have to subtract $50 from another category, but it shouldn't take much effort to find a category to save in. Seriously, for many of us, $50 is *one meal* at a restaurant on the weekend. Cook that one meal at home instead, and stash your savings away. It can be as simple as that!

But I Need More!

You might be reading this and saying to yourself, "Three hundred dollars wouldn't begin to pay for my holiday gifts!" Maybe it wouldn't, but wouldn't that amount at least help you get a good start? I chose $300 because $50 is a fairly reasonable amount to save up without hurting my month too much. But that's also the amount I chose because it works for my family and me. If you work really hard, perhaps you can double your savings and have $600 at the end of November. That's $100 a month you would have to save in order to meet that goal.

If you don't even know how you will swing $50 a month, try scaling back to $30 instead. Take these tips and make them work for you! Make them your own and you'll come back to them over and over again because they will help you save more money.

If you're someone who doesn't think you can make a dent in your holiday budget with $300 or even $600, is it time to scale back your holiday spending overall? Some of the most meaningful gifts you'll ever give and receive are those that come from the heart. You know the gifts I'm talking about. Maybe your grandma knit you a beautiful baby blanket for your new son or daughter. A friend gave you a themed package that fits your personality perfectly. Your neighbor left some fresh-baked cookies in a festive tin on your front door.

Those are the kinds of gifts that we most remember and cherish. When it's all said and done, the holidays are about being with the ones we love and celebrating life's beautiful moments. Gifts are just an enhancement. If you're feeling overwhelmed by all the gifts you need to give, maybe it's time to pare down the list and give more meaningful gifts from the heart.

What about January?

If you follow this tip and faithfully put back at least $50 a month from June to November, you'll probably relish the feeling of having cash to spend for some or all of your holiday gifts. It will make you proud to set a goal, work on it a little each month, and accomplish it. So what happens after you've had a wonderful holiday using cash and January rolls along? Should you just return to your old ways of not stockpiling money since December is now twelve months off?

Why not challenge yourself to continue saving $50 a month or whatever amount you decided on and stockpile again until June? You're already in the habit of saving the money, so it shouldn't be too difficult to continue. This time you can decide where you want the money to go. How about a vacation fund? That $300 could potentially pay for a couple of nights in a hotel or be used as spending money on the trip. The important thing to remember is that you've established a good habit, so it's only going to serve you well to continue practicing it. Then when June comes along, begin saving again for the holidays in December.

How It Worked for Me

I have been planning to try this tip since last Christmas when I *didn't* have any cash set aside for gifts. So I was really excited to get started when June rolled around. By now, both June and July have passed and I am excited to say, I am right on track with my Christmas saving! I have $100 set aside and will continue adding to it during the months of August through November. The trick for me has been to set the money aside as close to the beginning of the month as possible. As the end of the month nears, I would probably be worried that I needed the money for something else, but setting it aside at the start of each month has been "out of sight, out of mind" for me. This is a tip I know I will use again and again.

Ready . . . Set . . . Save

- Depending on what month it is when you read this chapter, you can either start saving for the holidays or saving for another goal, such as an upcoming vacation. But start now so you can get in the habit of setting aside some money each month for any costly upcoming events. You will thank yourself later!

- Decide on the amount that you will save each month. If you're just trying it out, I recommend $50. It's not a whole lot, but enough to allow you to stockpile some serious cash by December.

- Decide where the money will come from. Will you earn it using your unique skill set and abilities? Or will you build it into your budget and take it from another category? The choice is yours, just as long as you save the money!

Bonus Chapter:

8 Awesome Holiday Savings Hacks

Ready to put more "Ho, Ho, Ho" in your holiday savings this year? Check out these money-saving ideas for the most wonderful time of the year!

- **Buy all your wrapping paper from the dollar store.** They actually have great selections, as long as you get it early (before Halloween!). The longer you wait, the more picked over it will be.

- **Have Christmas after Christmas.** Stuff goes on deep discount on December 26. Yes, you run the risk of lower stock, but you'll practically have the mall to yourself, and you won't have to pay full price for many items!

- **Establish a spending limit with those you exchange gifts with.** Have an honest conversation with extended family and friends about what you can all actually afford to spend on gifts for each person. It's also ok to decide not to exchange gifts and simply enjoy one another's company.

- **Visit your favorite thrift stores for decorations and quirky gifts that are one of a kind.** Many thrift stores have a full aisle dedicated to holiday decorations. There are treasures and bargains to be found if you look hard enough.

- **Make a giant batch of holiday cookies** and divide them by the dozen to give away to neighbors, teachers, coworkers, people who provide services to you through the year, etc. Most everyone appreciates a box of baked goodness! And even if they can't eat it, they can surely find someone who can. It's the thought that counts!

- **Put your special skills to work by printing and gifting coupons for free services.** Whether it's music lessons, babysitting, or organizing, gift your friends and family with your services and encourage them to use the service!

- **Set a holiday budget and stick with it!** Have a family meeting and make sure everyone knows that you're going to spend a certain number of dollars and after it's gone, it's gone. Brainstorm creative, inexpensive gifts that will mean something to the recipients and set a spending limit for each person on the list.

- **Shop for the holidays all year long.** Always keep some extra cash on hand for buying presents. When you see that item your sister would love go on sale in February, you'll be able to snatch it up and have a great gift when December arrives.

Chapter 8: Creative Savings #6: Buy It Used

One family who has always intrigued me is the Duggar family of the *19 Kids and Counting* fame. I enjoyed watching their show on TLC when it aired, if for nothing more than to see how their crazy-big family got things done. They have their daily schedule down to a science. It's difficult for me to get one toddler-aged child out the door; I can't even wrap my mind around nineteen!

The Duggars seem to know a thing or two about saving money. The last I checked, one online report said that the Duggar family had a net worth of about $3.5 million! They are definitely doing something right with money. On the show, the older kids often went shopping for "new" clothes, heading to their favorite thrift stores. They don't buy new clothes often because they are either using their older siblings hand-me-downs or buying gently used clothing from the thrift store. And they don't seem to mind it at all.

In Jim Bob and Michelle Duggar's book, *A Love That Multiplies*, they discuss how they came to live in their current house. They do not have a mortgage, but bought the land and built the house as they had the money to do it. In fact, they said that it took several years to have air conditioning installed in the house because they waited until they had the cash money to pay for it! Talk about delayed gratification!

One of the phrases the parents teach their children is "buy used and save the difference." They encourage their children to compare prices on the same item, both new and used and purchase the used item and save the difference that it would have cost to purchase the new item.

That is the savings tip we're going to cover in this chapter: buying used. Just how much money can you save buying used? Let's take the journey together and find out!

Buy Used . . .

You can save a lot by buying used items, but there's no need to be overwhelmed by jumping in full-force. Let's get your feet wet instead, by choosing a category and trying out the buying-used principle there.

First, think of a category of goods in which you would like to save some money. This is an easy one for me. I love buying and reading books. But the bookstore prices are often more than I want to pay. I do, however, like to visit my local bookstore to find new titles that interest me. I browse, select a few titles, and then I put them back. This drives my husband crazy, by the way. He doesn't understand the purpose of going to the bookstore in the first place and spending all that time browsing if I'm not going to purchase anything!

I usually only purchase titles if I get them at a deep discount. I like books to be under the $10 price tag and then I'll consider them. If there is a book I want that is full retail, I come home and find it online. I research what the cost would be to buy it as an ebook versus buying it used in hardback or paper format and having it shipped. Sometimes I don't buy the book at all, but wait to see if I really want it. I can't tell you how many times I've been browsing at a thrift store and found the very book that was full retail price at the bookstore sitting on a thrift store shelf for fifty cents! Saving on books is an area where I could potentially pocket a lot of savings because I purchase them often.

Maybe books aren't your thing, but perhaps you are a fashionista and like buying clothes. You can definitely save big bucks by buying used clothes. Thrift stores are a great place to start. There have been many times when I've needed to put together a quick costume and don't want to shell out full price, so I run to the thrift store and piece one together with different finds. Thrift stores have great bargains and lots of treasures, if you don't mind hunting for them. And they are constantly getting in "new" stuff, so their selection will vary from day to day.

Another place to acquire used clothing is at a garage or yard sale. I've noticed that clothes don't seem to sell that well at yard sales, so if you are in the market for clothes, you might want to wait until later on in the day and offer one price for the bulk of clothes (if there are enough pieces you actually like). Just like the thrift shop, you can find many treasures at a yard sale. And don't be afraid to use your negotiating skills. Most of the time, people are just eager to clear out some of their junk.

Another place to consider buying gently used, nice clothing is at a consignment shop. If you're into brand-name items, consignment stores are the place to look. Sure, they are going to be a bit more expensive than thrift stores, but will still *usually* be cheaper than department store prices. I say usually because every once in a while, major department stores runs incredible sales (such as at the end of each season) where you can get fantastic prices on new clothing that is soon to be out of season. So, if you shop at your favorite department store and want to save big, consider stocking up for seasons to come and you'll get the best deals.

We already discussed ways to save on food in an earlier chapter, so I won't go into a big discussion about grocery savings here. Obviously, you can't buy "used" food; that's just gross to even think about! But you can look for deep sales at discount grocery stores on items you use often. Or consider buying store brand as opposed to name brand, if a particular item is worth the savings of buying it generic. We usually buy most of our over-the-counter medication in store brand because for our family, it works just as much as paying almost double for the name brand. That's an area where you can rack up huge savings if it works for you to purchase store brand.

Furniture is another major area of potential savings. Think about how much you typically spend for a new piece of furniture: anywhere from several hundred bucks to thousands of dollars! Are you in the market for new furniture? Is it something you would consider buying used?

I know a couple who recently moved into their new home, but because the size of their space increased, they needed some additional furniture to fill it. When my husband and I went over to their home months later, they gave us the grand tour and the husband said, "We bought all of our furniture gently used online for dirt cheap!" I was impressed because the furniture wasn't your run-of-the-mill secondhand furniture with a bunch of nicks and marks in it. It was nice stuff! This couple found pleasure in furniture shopping on a popular website for local secondhand stuff. And who knows how many hundreds of dollars they saved, all while furnishing their new house.

Hopefully you've now come up with a category you'd like to try out the "buy used" principle with, whether it be books, clothing, furniture, or some other category. Once you've figured it out, it's time to compare prices between the new and used. When comparing prices, you might have to estimate as opposed to trying to figure out the exact amount you would save, especially if you're buying a used product that's not the exact replica of a new item.

Let's take the example of a book. When I was expecting my son, there was a popular book on pregnancy that I wanted to purchase. I immediately went to my favorite thrift store and purchased a near-new copy for $.50. Today, if I were to go to my local bookstore and purchase the same book new, I would pay $14.95 retail. If I bought it online at my favorite online bookstore, I would pay $8.18 plus $3.99 in shipping, totaling $12.17. That's a little better than paying full retail, but doesn't even come close to paying fifty cents!

By comparing costs, I saved $11.67–$14.45 by buying used! If I tried to purchase more books at that price and compared them to what I would normally pay retail or online (new), I could save a lot of money over time.

Save the Difference

Buying used is only the first part of the equation; in order to benefit from this savings tip, you've got to actually save the difference. Remember how I said earlier that if you don't have a plan for your money, it will leave and you'll have no idea where it went? Whether you save $15 or $150 using the "buy used" principle, it won't do your savings account any good if you don't pocket the difference. Here is a surefire way to make sure that money gets in your savings.

Once you've determined an item you'd like to purchase, research the full price. That is the price you will "pretend" you are paying for the item. You will want the full amount in cash for your purchase. Locate the used item, whether it be online or in a store. Purchase the item, using the cash. Whatever you have leftover will be set aside for savings. You can either put the cash into an envelope designated for savings or take it to your bank and deposit it.

This technique will also work if you're paying with a debit card. You would allot the total price for the item, purchase it used with a card and then have the difference between the new and used item directly deposited into your savings. The only reason I recommend the cash method is because it will feel more real to you to actually hold the cash in your hand that you saved.

Either way, it's a simple process of getting the item(s) you want and saving at the same time.

Don't Do This

I couldn't write a chapter on buying used items without including a warning that it is possible to take the "buying used" principle too far. Let's be honest; there are some items you just shouldn't buy used. Undergarments, for instance, should not be bought used. I don't even think thrift stores should carry them, but I'm sure they're not going to listen to me. If you think you are desperate enough to buy someone's used underwear, start back at the beginning of this book, save some money for a few months, and go buy yourself some new panties! I mean, seriously, they aren't that expensive.

I have to include a personal story that I'm not eager to tell, but at least it's good fodder for a book on savings. I learned the hard way that some things are just not worth buying used, even if you can save a ton of money.

About a year ago, I was a nursing mom. Even though I had a perfectly good pump that my sister-in-law so graciously lent to me, I really wanted my own. The kind of pump I used was a top-of-the-line, double-electric version, retailing (even now) about $250. I did not want to pay that. So, I went online, searching for, you guessed it, a gently used breast pump.

Well, I found one from an owner who said it was in great condition and had only been used six months. She was willing to include all the attachment parts, which of course I didn't need because I had my own. The best part was that the picture looked exactly like the one I was currently borrowing. And the asking price was only $65! On paper, that looked great! I was saving $185 that could be used for other things. And I would have a pump of my own that I could use with my future babies.

I arranged to drive to the woman's house and pick up the pump. I took my mother-in-law with me just in case anything was sketchy and we needed a quick getaway. I don't know what we would have done exactly, but I guess I figured there was strength in numbers! We arrived at the house and the woman let me in. She was very nice and introduced me to her cute little daughter.

Then she showed me the pump. It was not the same as the one I had, even remotely. Although it was the same brand, it was a much older version that looked like it had been through some storms. She turned it on to show me that it worked and it made the most horrifying noise. I really didn't want to hand over my cash money, but I felt obligated. I guess, in retrospect, I could have calmly explained to her that the product was not what I thought I was purchasing and hoped she let me out of the deal, but I wanted to save face with her, with my mother-in-law waiting patiently in the car, and with my husband, whom I'd gone to great lengths to convince that buying a used breast pump was a good idea! So, I forked over the money and took the decrepit pump home. Once at home, I tried it out and it didn't work nearly as well as the one I was borrowing.

I learned my lesson. That pump is currently in my pile of things to take to charity. I didn't save $185. I basically threw away $65. And the next time I have another baby, I'll be purchasing a brand new, top-of-the-line pump from the store (hopefully with coupons)!

The moral of this story is that sometimes, no matter how good the deal seems, you need to buy brand new items. I hope you'll take my word for it on this one and save yourself the trouble of wasting money on certain used items. If you're in doubt about whether or not to buy a certain item used, it might be best to save up and buy it new!

How It Worked for Me

I'll admit, I've fallen off the bandwagon with this savings tip. Meaning, I've bought many used books since I wrote the chapter, but failed to deposit the difference I've saved into my account. I think I just need to remind myself that I need to set aside my savings when I buy used books and I will be much more successful. I know there is potential for great savings with this tip.

Ready . . . Set . . . Save

- Instead of trying to save on everything (although some people are skilled and successful at that), choose one category to try out the "buy used and save" principle. We discussed books, clothes, and furniture here, but I'm sure you can come up with your own meaningful category if none of these appeal to you.

- To make this tip work, you actually have to buy an item at the discounted price and save the difference. Make sure you have the full retail price set aside first (preferably in cash), then pay for the item and save the money left over.

- To amp up your savings, track your spending in a category for one month. Keep a running tally of the money you've saved by buying used and celebrate your awesome savings skills when the dollars add up at the end of the month!

Chapter 9: Creative Savings #7: The $5 Ban

I don't know how I survived before Pinterest came along! I never even knew about the amazing website until I saw a friend scrolling through it on her phone one day. She was looking at nail polish colors and leaned over to get my opinion on a shade. I was instantly intrigued with the app and asked her what it was. "Oh, it's Pinterest, and you should totally sign up for it." So I went home and opened a Pinterest account. And the rest, as they say, is history.

I'm not a crazy-obsessive Pinterest user who is on the site at all hours of the day, but I do check it every once in a while and have used it quite successfully to help navigate planning areas of my life. When I was pregnant with my son, I started a board about babies and was able to plan and pin most of the furniture and décor that is now in his nursery. Like many users, I also have a recipe board, and whenever I need a fresh idea for dinner or a decadent dessert, I visit that board.

Another board I started focuses on saving money. Since I am a frequent couponer, I might need to save a post for a deeply discounted product to remind myself to pick it up that week. I also save money tips in general on this board. In fact, it was my money board that got the wheels turning in my head for this book! I realized that the money-saving tips I read seemed to be all the same, and I wanted some unique, creative ways to save.

However, there was one tip I kept coming back to on Pinterest because it's simple and quite brilliant in my opinion, so I won't take credit for it at all. This tip is the $5 ban. It's a simple tip that has the power to grow your savings stash like a wildfire!

Spend-Me-Not

From now on, you're going to need to picture every $5 bill you encounter with big, bold, blood-red words written across it:

"SPEND ME NOT."

Ok, so that was a little dramatic, even for me. This savings tip is deceptively simple though; don't spend any $5 bill that comes into your possession. Instead put it aside and save it. Even though it's a simple tip, do you have the willpower to do it? I know for me, it will be a challenge to withhold my $5 bill when faced with the temptation of my favorite iced coffee. I'm going to have to be savvy and bring one-dollar bills instead.

With other tips in this book, I've covered storage of all your saved cash. I've talked about decorated envelopes or moneyboxes. I've mentioned using see-through jars and piggy banks of all shapes and sizes. For this tip, you will have to decide the best option that works for you. If you think you'll be tempted to pull out your fives anytime you need some cash, perhaps the best option is a lockbox. Also, depending on how long you follow this tip, you'll probably need more space for your cash than just an envelope. I might start out using a glass jar for my $5's and move some of the cash to a different place if the jar starts getting too full. What a nice problem that would be!

Delayed Gratification for a Year?

The time limit on this tip varies. How long can you delay gratification and avoid spending any $5 bill that comes your way? I read two quick blog posts about people who have successfully used this savings tip. Both of them were able to stash their $5's for a year! I know it seems like a long time to not spend those fives, but wait until you find out what they saved. One woman reported saving $1,300 in that year. The other person saved more than $3,000, just by stockpiling her fives! What do you think accounts for the difference between their savings? Simply put, the one who saved $3,000 probably uses more cash than the one who saved $1,300.

If you can do it, delayed gratification for a year can increase your savings by not just hundreds of dollars, but thousands! That might make it worth the wait to you.

Inviting Other Presidents

Before you think that this savings party is just limited to Honest Abe (the face on the $5 bill), let me encourage you that you could try inviting other presidents to the party too, but Mr. Lincoln seems like the easiest to start with.

Let's face it; Mr. Washington ($1 bill) is just too common. We will probably need him on a day-to-day basis (remember my iced coffee scenario). So I wouldn't recommend stockpiling your $1's for this particular tip. Use those for your every-day transactions and be sure to save your change.

But maybe you're the ambitious type and would rather spend your Lincolns and save your Hamiltons instead. Every time you put back a $10, you are effectively doubling the savings you would have made if you had saved $5's. By the way, Alexander Hamilton wasn't a president, but still a pretty important man in US history as he was the first secretary of the Treasury. So even though he never lived in the White House, he can still be invited to the president's party if you want him to be.

I think the reason most people use the five-dollar bill with this savings tip (or spending ban, if you really think about it) is because it is neither too small nor too large.

The amount isn't so small that it would take you years on end to save thousands of dollars. If you chose to never spend a dollar bill, and hold back one every single day, it would still take you years before you had $1,000. But those fives can add up quickly. They are also not so large that you would necessarily miss them the way you would a ten or twenty.

How It Worked for Me

I was excited to start this particular experiment in saving my fives. I don't know if it was the prospect of saving some serious cash or the motivating picture of all of those $5's stacked together on Pinterest.

I placed a pretty glass jar on my formal dining room table where I will see it often and started putting $5's in it. To be honest, I've gotten off track several times because I've had to make change when someone pays me for a music lesson. But, my jar is still steadily filling up with fives, which is a step in the right direction. I get a thrill every time I look at that jar. What can I say? It makes me feel rich!

Ready . . . Set . . . Save

- If you would like more information about this savings tip, do some Internet research to find out about people who have used it successfully. You can look on Pinterest because there are several versions of the tip floating around there, or you can search online for "five dollar ban" and see what results you find.

- Once you've decided what denomination you want to "ban," determine your timeline for saving. Most people have had success with stretching the ban out for one year, but if you don't think you can delay gratification that long, try it for several months or even half a year. By the end of your timeline, count your money, relish your savings, and you might just feel like continuing the ban through the year!

- Because this savings tip has the potential to net you some serious cash, set a goal for your savings at the end of the timeline. You could use the cash to pay extra on your debt, take a vacation, or buy passes to your local amusement park. Just make sure you have a clearly defined purpose for the money and you'll be more likely to save all you can.

Chapter 10: Creative Savings #8: Pantry Raid 'n' Save

By now, you have been introduced to seven creative tips on saving money. Some of them will save you a little; some of them can save you serious cash. All of them have the potential to boost your savings overall and get you on the road to living your dreams and achieving your goals.

The last tip might be one of the most creative of all: the Pantry Raid 'n' Save. This savings tip is guaranteed to be fun for the whole family. You don't even have to tell them that the goal is to save money! Just tell them that you are going on a treasure hunt for dinner and they are responsible for gathering the spoils.

In the first savings tip, I showed you how to take your weekly grocery store savings and add that to your actual savings account or cash fund. This tip ties in with that, but will help you in a pinch when you need to save $100–$200 quickly. It will require you to get creative in the kitchen, while likely yielding lots of laughter and fun memories when you look back.

Must Have Food

The pantry raid will require that you already have some food in your pantry. If you open it up and your shelves are bare, this is not the time to try this tip! You need to print some coupons, look at your local grocery store circulars, and load up on good deals. Once your pantry is somewhat stocked with the basics, then this tip will serve you well. Let the creativity begin!

Do you ever have those days when you rush through the day from activity to activity, planning on taking the time to figure out dinner, and then magically, 5:30pm is upon you and you never got around to planning dinner, much less make it? It's too late to try out a new recipe and you don't want to resort to going through a drive-through—again. This is not the time to panic. This is the perfect time for a pantry raid.

Mission: Dinner

Call your children, your significant other, or your cat to the kitchen. Tell them that you have a mission and it is their job to help you complete it. It's called "Mission: Dinner" and it needs to be on the table in t-minus thirty minutes. They can pull ingredients from the pantry, fridge, and freezer to come up with a meal plan, but everyone has to agree that they will at least try eating the dinner or the mission will be a failure. This is why it's so important that everyone choose ingredients that others in the family will eat.

Start a timer if you wish and unleash your team to complete the mission. Let them rush around like the chefs in *Chopped* and gather chosen ingredients in a common spot (such as the counter), so everyone knows what they're working with. Give everyone a job as you cook and serve the meal together. Yes, even the little ones can dump frozen veggies in a pot or stir a bowl of fruit salad. When the timer goes off, your meal should be on the table, ready to be eaten. It will probably be one of the most memorable and enjoyable meals of your life, even if it doesn't taste like it came from a gourmet-cooking magazine. And you can bet if you have children, they will ask you to do it again!

How Will It Help Me Save?

Besides the obvious ways you will save, such as avoiding the dinner rush at the supermarket for expensive ingredients or shelling out your money at the closest drive-through, you will be using ingredients that might be gathering dust (eew!) on your shelves or that might have to be thrown out if you wait too long to use them. As we all know, throwing out unused food and ingredients you paid for at one time is like throwing your hard-earned dollars in the trash. The pantry raid allows you to clean your shelves and use food and ingredients that need to be used.

If you have a well-stocked pantry, fridge, and freezer, you can turn the pantry raid into a weeklong experience. This is where you'll really have the potential to save big because you are eliminating a weekly grocery trip. I don't know about you, but in my household, we easily spend more than $100 on groceries for the week. And that is after coupons and loyalty card savings. I've just resigned myself to the fact that we are going to spend at least that much and align my budget accordingly. To not have to go to the store one week out of a month would save us hundreds of dollars.

A weeklong pantry raid will help you purge your kitchen of any extra items that you need to use. Just be aware ahead of time that after a week of eating from the groceries you already have on hand, you will have to plan a grocery trip to restock your pantry staples.

Organizing the Pantry Raid

If you go into this savings tip organized, it will save you many headaches about missing ingredients that you might need to put together meals for the family. Of course, you don't have to share with anyone the fact that you planned ingredients to be strategically placed in the pantry. You can just keep that secret to yourself, and take all the credit for magically having lots of versatile ingredients on hand for breakfast, lunch, and dinner.

The easiest way to organize a future pantry raid is to take time to think about the main ingredients that go into your favorite meals. Let's say, for instance, your family loves spaghetti and meatballs. You can pre-stock your kitchen with basic ingredients needed to pull together that meal: pasta noodles, pasta sauce, and frozen meatballs. If you buy a loaf of French bread that needs to be used up, you can make a simple dressing for it using butter and garlic salt or powder, pop it in the oven for a few minutes, and you've got an easy garlic bread to accompany the entrée.

Or, the same ingredients could be used to make meatball sandwiches instead. Take away the pasta, and hollow out the bread to add your meatballs cooked in sauce, smothered with whatever white cheese you have on hand: mozzarella, provolone, or even shredded parmesan.

If you have sandwich bread that needs to be used up and plenty of eggs in the fridge, you could whip up a quick vanilla-infused French toast by adding vanilla extract and a dash of cinnamon to the egg-and-milk mixture. Cut up whatever fruit you have on hand to accompany the toast and you've got an easy breakfast, lunch, or dinner, depending on the time of day!

Many times, your favorite meals can be created or duplicated using staple ingredients you have on hand. But I think the best part about the pantry raid is that when it becomes a family affair, you will all tend to be more creative and combine ingredients that you wouldn't have considered on your own. This savings tip is all about saving money, but it's also about bringing back a trait that is lost in so many American households today: resourcefulness.

What happens if you run out of something at your house? Do you dash off to the closest store to pick it up? Convenience is a key element in our lives today, and while it's nice to be able to visit the mega-market that stays open twenty-four hours a day, we've lost the element of creativity by using what's already on hand. That's probably why I like this tip so much, because it gets me thinking outside the box. And when I'm thinking outside the box, who knows what cool ideas I might come up with next!

A Shining Example

The whole time I've been writing this chapter, I've been thinking of my dad, who is not only a naturally resourceful guy, but also a master of the pantry raid tip. My dad currently has a little apartment in Pennsylvania, and if he's not commuting to and from work, he's either finding furniture for his apartment, building or repairing furniture for his apartment, or preparing a meal using the pantry raid method described here.

He doesn't use the pantry raid because he has to; he uses it because he likes to be creative in the kitchen and doesn't like to see food go to waste.

I'm going to describe some of his actual meals, just to get your creative juices flowing. Though some of his concoctions are, well, unusual, he is really good at combining foods that you wouldn't think go together at all.

Here's one post from my dad's social media page:

"Guac night! Made fresh guacamole with nectarine and garlic, cilantro, lemon juice, and paprika. Served with a jar of salsa with a dash of sour cream. It was awesome. You need to make some immediately."

When someone made the comment that it was creative to think of including nectarine in the guacamole, my dad's reply was, "It's what I happened to have on hand that night. Turned out pretty good though." Can you say Pantry Raid Master or what?

Another time, he wanted to use his leftover hotdogs, but didn't have any hot-dog buns on hand, so he simply placed the franks on top of regular sandwich bread and dressed them with his favorite condiments of chopped onion, mustard, ketchup, and pickle relish. He posted a picture on his social media page and called the meal, "Hotdogs in a Blanket."

Even though I've read about many people using the pantry raid tip with success, my dad brought it to life for me because he practices the tip so well. One thing is for sure: he never runs out of creative ideas in the kitchen by using his ingredients on hand, and he's not afraid to combine them in unusual ways!

How It Worked for Me

I started incorporating this tip by thinking about my family's favorite meals. My son and I enjoy anything with pasta and cheese, so those are two categories I keep well stocked in my pantry and fridge. My husband prefers a protein (such as boneless chicken breasts) and a vegetable side. So I also tend to keep frozen chicken and packages of vegetables in the freezer that can be conveniently turned into quick dinners.

While we haven't skipped a week of buying groceries up to this point, we have been able to cook many meals at home instead of resorting to eating out, simply because we've stocked our kitchen with versatile ingredients that we like. I look forward to trying the weeklong pantry raid soon.

Ready . . . Set . . . Save

- Have a family meeting and come up with your top three favorite dishes for each category: breakfast, lunch, dinner, and snacks. Make a master list that includes ingredients for all the dishes. Bonus points if you can use the same ingredient in multiple meals! Keep the list basic, and keep it with you in case you catch ingredients at a great buy while shopping. You might even think about adding it as a memo to your phone. Referring to this list and purchasing the items on it will help you stock your pantry, fridge, and freezer for a future pantry raid.

- If your local supermarket has buy one, get one (BOGO) free deals on your ingredients from your master list, be sure to take advantage. Buy once, eat twice!

- Once your kitchen is well stocked, try out the pantry raid for one week. Don't be afraid to use leftovers and repurpose them in different meals. Leftover veggies could become the basis for a hearty soup. Shredded chicken could be used in a cool chicken salad one day for lunch, followed by baked chicken enchiladas for dinner the next night. Take the limits off your imagination and see what great meals you

and your family can come up with.

Chapter 11: Putting It All Together

If you've stuck with me throughout this book, you've read eight of the most creative savings tips I could find. I'm not claiming to have created these myself, but I have made them my own, which is why I reported on how they worked for me at the end of each chapter.

Now, the spotlight is on you. It's time for you to decide which of these tips will work for you and make a plan of action. It's time to start saving and paying for your dreams. You have to take these tips and adapt them to meet your needs and goals. You and I don't think alike, so we won't save money alike. You can probably find many other creative ways to save; this book is just a tool to get you started and to help you think a little differently.

Many people are bemoaning the fact that they can't make enough money to survive. I challenge that thinking by suggesting that not only can we live beneath our means, but we can also thrive by saving part of our income and create a lasting legacy for our families.

To put these savings tips into action, all you really need to do is just get started. Listed below are the eight creative ways to save outlined in this book. Put a star by the ones that might work for you.

My 8 Ways to Save

- Grocery shopping savings

- Habit building and savings

- Piggy bank party

- Percentage savings plan

- Christmas in June savings

- Buy it used

- The $5 ban

- Pantry raid 'n' save

- Bonus: automated savings

There are really nine ways to save if you count the automated savings, but that one is so important and easy to do that I had to include it. Of the tips that you starred, what is one tip that you could most likely get started on *today*? Yes, I am challenging you to get started today. Time waits for no one and you have no idea what the future holds. The only time you have is the present, so why not start saving your money now? Complete this sentence:

The one savings tip that I can start working on today is

Think about how you will put this tip into action. What materials and supplies do you need to make it happen? How will you customize it to fit with your lifestyle? Keep in mind that the guidelines are just that: guidelines. There's no rule that says you have to do it my way or it won't work. In fact, it probably won't work well for you if you do it my way because we are not the same person.

Find your own way to make these tips work for you, and you will probably start saving more money than you ever have before because you're not following a formula. Instead, you're creating a system of handling your money that is tailor-made for you and your family.

Different tips presented in this book use different time frames. Some can help you save quickly in one month; others need to be spread out over several months for you to see real results. Let's say you start with a tip that only requires a month to start seeing your savings pile up. You try out the tip, and you fail. Let me give you a hint: when you're changing habits and doing things differently, you will fail. A lot. And guess what? That's ok. What's not ok is to give up and go back to status quo. You have to keep trying. If one tip didn't work the way you hoped, how can you rework it and try again? Or maybe you need to put that one on pause and try out a different one. The next one might work much better for you.

Ideally, if you want to see some significant growth of your savings, you can try several of these tips simultaneously, and commit to the process during the course of a year. I know that sounds daunting, but if you break it down, it's not that bad. How quickly does a year pass anyway? One day you're making those ever-popular new year's resolutions; the next day, it seems, it's summer vacation. Fairly soon, it's time to serve Thanksgiving dinner, and before you know it, December 31 rolls around again. A year goes by quickly.

Why not challenge yourself to spend the next year growing your savings like never before? Get your entire family on board and you'll have others to motivate you when you get discouraged and are tempted to quit.

Even if you choose only three tips to try during the next year, your potential for savings could be great. Say in January, you decide to start with the buying used tip.

1

You choose the category of clothing and only buy clothing that is either deeply discounted or from your favorite thrift store. You save $60 by buying used (or new clothing on clearance) in January.

2

At the same time, you put a giant piggy bank in your child's bedroom and tell her that you are going to start feeding the pig all your silver change for the next six months. You get her excited about it and she ends her daily routine by feeding the pig. In six months, the bank is almost full, so you get some coin wrappers and have a "piggy party" with the family. Your coins saved during six months add up to $120!

3

Meanwhile, you decide to use the $5 ban tip during the course of the entire year, and your partner also does it with you. Every time one of you has a $5 bill in your possession, you put it aside into a metal moneybox. At the end of the year, you add up all the $5's you've saved and your total comes to $1,850!

Now, let's pretend that you only practiced these three tips because that's all you had time for in the year. During 365 days, with some effort but not exhausting yourself, you've managed to save $2,030, just by trying a few of these creative savings tips. That doesn't even take into account the savings you could include if you did the automatic savings tip covered at the beginning of the book. Now imagine with me for a second, how much glorious savings you could have if you tried all the tips and even added some of your own!

Right now, there are some annoying weeds growing up through the cracks on my back patio. In fact, most of the patio is covered with the little sprouts. But it didn't start out that way. Those weeds started out barely peeking above the bricks. Even several weeks ago, I didn't even notice them. But give them a little sun and rain, and now they are really adding up.

Even though this is an example of something I don't want to grow, the point is, your savings can start small. A little here, a little there, and it soon adds up to something much bigger than you ever anticipated. If you are someone who doesn't think you have a lot to save, just get started anyway. I bet you will be surprised at what grows out of a few coins here and a few bills there.

When you start to see progress, it motivates you to continue on the journey, maybe even going farther down the road than you originally intended. Before you know it, you are well on your way to living the life of your dreams! All because you started with what you had and allowed it to grow and flourish.

Creative Savers

I didn't want to write a book on savings with just my own ideas about how to creatively grow your money. In fact, this book wouldn't be in your hands (or on your phone or tablet) without the contributions of many creative savers and their fabulous ideas. I conducted some research on social media and asked some of my friends for their best and most creative savings tips. Here are five of my favorite responses:

~~~~~

"I sign up on email listings for stores and restaurants I enjoy. They often send special discounts for birthdays/anniversaries in addition to coupons for members only. Also, if there is a product I really enjoy, I send a message to the company letting them know. They will often send coupons or freebies as a thank you."

—Holly from Kentucky

"We eat out based on when restaurants run happy hour specials on appetizers. I also sign up for every single e-club out there and get tons and tons of free stuff for my birthday. With my birthday in June, we live practically all of June and July off of my birthday coupons . . . free food everywhere! I get about 50+ free meals/desserts/great discounts just off my birthday."

—Cheryl from Florida

"I wanted to try hot yoga but didn't want to spend the money on membership, so I learned how to do a lot of the moves from various videos and apps, and then bought a yoga mat and started taking it to the gym (that I was already paying for) with me and set it up in the sauna. Now I have my own hot yoga class and only pay for one membership!"

—Kacy from Kentucky

"I'm not a great saver, but one thing I do is stash away one-dollar bills! Anytime my husband or I have one, I stick it in a drawer . . . they add up quick! The same goes for coins!"

—Tracy from Florida

"Friends don't let friends buy retail . . . you can usually purchase the same or similar items with big discounts at resale and consignment shops . . . everything from furniture to clothes to household and decorative items. Also check Amazon and eBay, especially for cosmetics and accessories."

—Linda from Florida

~~~~~

I am completely inspired by my fellow creative savers out there and their great tips. It doesn't matter how you save, just that you do it. No matter what kind of income you have, you can always find creative ways to stretch your dollars and hold back some savings. All the tips from my friends are creative, and none of them require large incomes or expensive supplies to get started.

The possibilities to save are all around you. All you have to do is choose one and get to it!

Bonus Chapter:
8 Great Savings Resources

When it gets hard to save, we all need a great support system to remind us of our purpose and help us to dream once again. If you are struggling to find inspiration, here are eight of my favorite resources that have helped me on my savings and money management journey.

- **Living Well, Spending Less:** This website is by the fabulous Ruth Soukup and includes tips on money management, decluttering, family life, cooking, and much more. Once a year in October, readers can sign up for "31 Days of Living Well and Spending Zero," which will really help to grow your savings. A bonus is that all her recipes I've ever tried are delicious, especially the hummingbird cake! Website: livingwellspendingless.com

- **Dave Ramsey:** A successful money management guru who has been through bankruptcy and back offers advice on money and business the world over. This website is also the home of the famous Financial Peace University, the program that leads families through the seven steps to achieve financial independence and success. If you need help with a budget, this website will take you step by step through creating a comprehensive monthly cash flow sheet. I have really enjoyed the success stories featured on Dave's weekday podcast. Website: daveramsey.com

- **Pinterest:** You've already heard my take on Pinterest from a previous chapter, so if you don't yet have an account, the best way to experience it is to sign up (it's free)! Pinterest allows you to pin any image from the Internet to online boards you create. You can also follow other pinners and send favorite pins to your friends. Website: pinterest.com

- **Dan Miller:** Dan Miller is a life coach known for helping people "find or create work that they love." The reason I include him in this list is because his books and podcasts will make you dream about meaningful work and he often gives tips about increasing your income. Start with his website for some awesome freebies: 48days.com

- **Feed the Pig:** This site is run by the American Institute of CPAs and includes information about everything from retirement to debt management to savings. It is home of the 4-Week Financial Fitness Challenge, which will help you come up with a five-year financial game plan. Website: feedthepig.org

- **Krazy Coupon Lady**: Welcome to the world of extreme couponing! This website claims to be the "world's #1 coupon site." If you've never experienced the thrill of getting free items from the store, this awesome site will show you how. It also includes weekly deals, informative how-to articles on saving just about everywhere, and cute YouTube videos. Just a warning: it's easy to spend an entire afternoon on this site! It's addicting. Website: thekrazycouponlady.com

- **Target Cartwheel**: I had to include this app on my list of resources because Target is not only my favorite store, but also the place my family buys weekly groceries. The app features percentage-off deals on many items that rarely have coupons: produce, meat, milk and other dairy products, electronics, and clothing. The more you use the app, the more spots you earn to add discounts. Simply install the app on your phone and have the barcode scanned at the register. You can use this app to get additional discounts after your coupons! Website: target.com (click on Target apps and find the Cartwheel app link).

- **Coupons.com**: This is the website to go to print manufacturer coupons for your favorite name-brand items. This site allows you to print the same coupon twice. You also don't have to sign in to access and print the coupons. Just make sure you have the print-plugin required (the site will walk you through installation) and plenty of paper and you're ready to print and go. Website: coupons.com

Chapter 12: The Dream Fund

You did it! Can you believe it? You've been working hard for a while now, bumped up your savings, and you're finally ready to fund some dreams! Before you get started with that, I hope you'll take the time to celebrate a job well done. You've done what many Americans have trouble doing: you've saved money for the future and now you have something to show for it. Pat yourself on the back and treat yourself and your family to a celebratory meal (with coupons, of course)!

If you're anything like me, you might be so enamored with your newfound ability to stockpile savings that you are tempted to keep it all hidden away, just in case you have a real emergency or there's a zombie apocalypse or something. But, the purpose of this book is to show you creative ways to save as a means to funding your dreams. The amazing part is now that you have mad savings skills, you'll be able to stockpile cash even faster the next time around. But right now, it's time to go out and spend some of that cash!

The Best Purchase I Ever Made

Back in college, I noticed that Apple computers were becoming popular, especially among people my age. What's ironic is when I was growing up, our household desktop computer was a Macintosh, but it was a terrible computer. It was extremely slow and crashed all the time. It wasn't easy to write papers on and I begged my dad to go mainstream and buy a PC. Didn't happen.

Then I went off to college and my parents purchased my first laptop, and I finally got my PC. It worked great and survived four years of school and numerous college writing assignments. By my senior year though, everyone around me had their swanky little MacBooks, which were just becoming en vogue. I found out that they were the best kind of computer for musicians to own and that many of the programs I needed to use as a professional were compatible with Apple. I determined that I would purchase one for myself once I was out of school and working enough to set aside some savings.

After graduation, I moved to Florida on a whim, and lived with a family who graciously gave me their spare bedroom and bathroom. I worked part-time at a local church as a music director and part-time as a barista at Starbucks. Those days, I really had nothing better to do than work, so I took all the hours I could and started cushioning my account.

I don't remember how long it took, but the money added up quickly and I was so excited to go online and shop for my computer. Instead of buying new, I discovered the refurbished models available and thought, "Why not?" So, I purchased a beautiful, new-to-me black MacBook with the cash I had saved up.

I used that computer for at least four years and never had any problems with it. I wrote books on that computer, created music, and thoroughly enjoyed my purchase. In fact, it stands out in my mind as the best purchase I ever made. Why? Because I had a goal to buy myself a computer and I saved up for it and achieved the goal.

Years down the road, my husband and I decided it was time to upgrade to a newer computer with more memory, and would you believe, I had offers from multiple people to buy my four-year old black MacBook? I ended up selling it for $300, which I was able to put toward the purchase of my new laptop. But I will always remember fondly that computer that I worked so hard for and bought with the money I saved.

The things and experiences that we sacrifice and save and eventually pay cash for are the ones we tend to appreciate the most. After all, we remember the work it took to get there. We may have had to forgo short-term pleasure for the long-term payoff, but in the process, we learn a valuable thing called patience. Patience builds character like nothing I've ever seen.

Write Your Own Story

As you prepare to fund the two goals you decided on at the beginning of this book, think about what your story will look like after all is said and done. Think about the things in your life that prompted you to choose the goals you did. Has it been years since your family went on vacation and now you're getting ready to spend a solid week traveling around the United States? How amazing will it feel to have that vacation that you've worked so hard for, over a year or maybe even longer?

If you're doing something you've always wanted to do, such as having laser surgery to correct your vision or finally getting the braces you never got as a kid, how incredible will it feel to see through "new eyes" for the first time or smile at yourself in the mirror with straight teeth? These are the moments you will remember. And if you're not quite ready to pay for them yet because you haven't saved up enough, these are the moments you need to think about to keep you motivated.

At some point in the journey, it will be easier to quit than to save another dollar. There will be a tiny purchase that beckons you to turn your focus away from your long-term goal. Only if you have the vision firmly planted in your head, will you be able to withstand and keep pressing forward when that time comes.

Save Now . . . Save Forever!

I hope that you've enjoyed the journey through this book with me. You had the chance to dream in the beginning and imagine what your life would look like as you achieved your two starter goals. You probably worked through some of the creative savings tips in the book and added your own unique flair to them. And if you stuck with saving for any length of time, you realized that you could, indeed, do it and watched with glee as your cash piled up. Maybe now, you're standing on the other side of a dream, one that you were able to pay cash for, and you're not sure what comes next.

Is it just me or does it sometimes feel like after a goal is achieved, there is a bit of a letdown? Ok, I just dropped twenty pounds, now what? I've come to expect and even welcome this emotion of achieving a dream and the feeling of not knowing where to go from here. It means that I've been hustling for a while on something that was important to me, and now that I've achieved it, it's time to dream again.

Once you've made it to this place, it's time for you too to dream again. Back to the drawing board, so to speak. Now that you know you can fund the life of your dreams, what are the next two goals that you'd like to tackle? Once you have the next goals in place, you can begin to devise a plan to save for them. You can use the same tips that worked so well for you the first time or change it up and try out some new ones. That's what's so great about this process: you get to choose! If you don't like your choice today, fine. Make a different one tomorrow.

Now that you have some creative savings skills and some success behind you, my hope is that you go confidently in the direction of your brightest future, knowing you can and will achieve all you set your mind to do.

Start a Revolution

The statistics for our country have a dismal story to tell. Credit card debt is increasing, due to our consumer, gotta-have-it-now mentality as a nation, in addition to credit being a product that is highly marketed everywhere we go. Don't believe me?

- The next time you watch your favorite show on television, do me a favor and count the number of credit card commercials that air during any given hour.

- If you're traveling by plane, pull out the in-flight magazine and look for the glossy, glamorous ad about the latest and greatest credit card.

- If you're traveling by car, I bet you'll see some credit card billboards dotting the freeways.

- Go visit your favorite department store and you'll be asked if you carry the store credit card when you purchase something.

Credit is being shoved in our faces everywhere.

As credit is booming, our pockets are emptying, and our savings are decreasing. You don't see advertisements for building a savings account, budgeting for the month, or establishing a solid emergency fund. Why? These things all take self-restraint and patience to do. Saving is not "sexy," because it requires delayed gratification for a little or a long while.

But you know what is sexy? Peace of mind that comes from not getting a giant credit card bill in the mail every month. The brilliance of the family who is living beneath their means and is enjoying their first vacation that they scrimped and saved and paid cash to go on. If you can learn the art of delaying gratification, your pay-off, literally and figuratively, is going to be so much bigger in the end.

As we come to the close of this book, I'm challenging you to go against the grain. Try it and see if you don't like it better than what the rest of the world seems to be doing. Put down the credit card, better yet, cut up the credit card or, at the very least, stop using it. Start telling your money where to go and allocate a little or a lot to savings. Dream some dreams, set some goals, and it won't be long until you are funding those same dreams that looked impossible and too costly at the start.

I hope to see you on the road less traveled. Be sure to wave hello! Maybe if enough of us travel this road, we will forge a new path and start a savings revolution!

Afterword: My Reflections on the Journey

This has been such an enjoyable book to work on! I have truly enjoyed writing every chapter and will be sorry to end it. Even though the book is done, the journey for me has only begun. The initial manuscript took me six solid months to write, but I hope I'll be reaping the benefits of saving money for years to come.

Here's an update on those two dreams I told you about in the beginning of this book: first, we decided to postpone our New York trip. Even though I was disappointed, I knew it was the right thing to do because I ended up making three separate trips to Nashville for some exciting music opportunities (I'll save that story for another book)! My plans changed, but the intensity of my savings did not as I worked to incorporate the tips I've discussed into my life.

My car is not yet paid off, but I am feeling hopeful as I have devised a plan to pay it off two years early and am currently paying extra on it each month. Also, I decided that a portion of the royalties from this book will go directly to paying off my car loan, so thank you so much for your support of this work! The most exciting part: once my car is paid off, our family will officially be debt-free, besides our house! I am looking forward to saving and paying cash for some big dreams once I write that final check for my car loan.

I hope this book has encouraged you to boost your savings effort with a little fun and creativity, no matter what your big dreams might be! I couldn't go on this journey without you, the reader, so please let me know how it's going. I would love to hear about your big dreams and what methods of saving you're using to fund them. And I would love your feedback on this book, whether sending me an email at jandkking@yahoo.com or leaving a review on Amazon. Remember, you are awesome, you are creative, and you can do this! Now go forth and save!

Kristin King
July 6, 2015

About the Author

Kristin King lives, loves, and saves with her husband, toddler son, and dog in Port Orange, Florida. She will be the first to admit that she has too many jobs, but loves them all. She is an elementary music teacher, business owner, and church music director but loves her most important roles as wife and mom. When she's not working on a writing project, she can probably be found in the kitchen baking something sweet or in her music room playing piano and singing.

A natural saver, Kristin wrote this book to challenge herself to become even more creative with her saving techniques in order to fund her own dreams of going on family vacations and becoming completely debt-free. As a result, she and her family are much closer to achieving both dreams. Kristin wanted to share what she's learned with others, hoping that they can find the same success!

Discover Other Titles by Kristin King